THE
IMPEACHMENT
OF GEORGE W. BUSH

THE IMPEACHMENT
OF GEORGE W. BUSH

A Handbook for Concerned Citizens

ELIZABETH HOLTZMAN
WITH CYNTHIA L. COOPER

Nation Books
New York

THE IMPEACHMENT OF GEORGE W. BUSH:
A Handbook for Concerned Citizens

Published by
Nation Books
An Imprint of Avalon Publishing Group, Inc.
245 West 17th Street, 11th Floor
New York, NY 10011

AVALON
publishing group incorporated

Nation Books is a co-publishing venture of the Nation Institute and Avalon
Publishing Group Incorporated.

Library of Congress Cataloging-in-Publication Data

ISBN-10: 1-56025-940-X
ISBN-13: 978-1-56025-940-4

9 8 7 6 5 4 3 2 1

Interior design by Maria E. Torres
Printed in the United States of America
Distributed by Publishers Group West

To Max:
A true friend of constitutional democracy
and an "enemy" of presidents
who are not

Contents

Why This Book:
Time to Begin

I stopped short when I saw a front page *New York Times* article about the Bush administration and domestic eavesdropping in late 2005. The story exposed a secret wiretapping program in the United States, set up with the approval of President Bush. Without court oversight, without judicial warrants, the domestic spying described by James Risen and Eric Lichtblau defied a federal statute. In the weeks following the mid-December publication, the president declared it was within in his power to authorize the program, despite the law. The president said he would continue to do so.

I experienced the same sick sensation in my stomach that I had during the Watergate hearings when I was a member of Congress, sitting on the House Judiciary Committee while we considered the impeachment of President Richard M. Nixon. Then, the flagrant abuse of our constitutional system at the hands of the president made an undeniable case for impeachment.

Now I was hearing George Walker Bush, president of the United States, declare that he had the right to eavesdrop on hundreds, possibly thousands or millions, of people in the United States without getting court approval. He claimed that right despite the prohibitions of the Federal Intelligence Surveillance Act and the Fourth Amendment of the U.S. Constitution.

Richard Milhous Nixon, when president, also engaged in illegal wiretaps. He, too, said it was for national security. He, too, put himself above the law. This formed one of the grounds for impeaching Nixon. Now I realized that it was time to look at President Bush in the same light.

With Nixon, the American people finally demanded that Congress act. The House of Representatives empowered the Judiciary Committee to begin an inquiry into presidential impeachment in late fall 1973. After months of careful work, a bipartisan majority of the thirty-eight committee members voted for the impeachment of President Nixon in July 1974. Ultimately all of the committee members, Democrats and Republicans, supported his impeachment.

We had many grounds for the impeachment of Nixon. Illegal wiretapping sat high on the list; misleading the public and abusing the powers of his office figured prominently.

The Judiciary Committee proceedings were thorough and fair. The grounds for impeachment were strong. As a result, Nixon resigned from office, the first president ever to do so. In resigning, he avoided becoming the first president ever to be removed from office.

I thought at that time that our work—careful and bipartisan—would send the strongest possible signal to future presidents about the need to obey the rule of law. I was wrong.

Thirty-three years later, the same issues, the same arrogance, the same abuse of power emanate from the White House, threatening our constitutional system. President Bush had completed one year of his second term when the illegal wiretapping scheme became public. The president's response was to carry on, regardless of the law against it and regardless of his constitutional duty to faithfully execute the laws of the United States. The only way to stop him is impeachment.

Having watched the unfolding of Watergate from the inner halls of Congress, I understood that the impeachment of President Bush wouldn't happen quickly. The American people need to evaluate the president's conduct and to recognize that his removal from office is the only way to preserve our democracy. People need an opportunity to see and hear and weigh the evidence. This book offers that possibility.

CHAPTER ONE

Setting the Stage:
Nixon, Watergate, and President Bush

THE MANY PHASES AND FACES OF "WATERGATE"

The break-in of Democratic Party national headquarters at the Watergate complex occurred in June 1972. Slowly, over time, this event set off a streak of inquiries into the impeachable misconduct of President Richard M. Nixon. Squelching investigations at first, Nixon was elected by one of the largest landslides in history in November 1972. The tipping point came sixteen months after the break-in when President Nixon forced the Watergate special prosecutor off the job. Nine months later, in July 1974, the House Judiciary Committee voted on three articles of impeachment. Ten days after the committee vote, Nixon resigned. The whole sequence of events took more than two years.

Today those activities feel collapsed into an instant. But in reality, "Watergate" is shorthand for dozens of incidents in addition to the break-in, involving a large cast of characters over a timeline of five and one-half years from 1969 to 1974.

The Nixon impeachment process proceeded deliberately and cautiously, driven by a deep belief in the preservation of our constitutional democracy. A brief tour of the events of Watergate is useful to understanding the impeachable offenses committed by President Bush.

Nixon's was the first impeachment proceeding since that of Andrew Johnson in the aftermath of the civil war. Historians overwhelmingly view the Johnson impeachment as a scandal, spawned by political hatred and fierce disagreement with Johnson's unwillingness, after the assassination of President Lincoln, to implement Reconstruction. Presidential historian Michael R. Beschloss describes it as a "craven, last-ditch move by political enemies." He wrote, "When the Senate began dealing with Andrew Johnson's impeachment in March 1868, the old chamber was turned into a near circus." The impeachment was set off when Johnson fired a cabinet member, in violation of a statute passed by Congress. Although the statute was later declared unconstitutional, the firing became the grounds for his impeachment. In a highly partisan process, the Senate failed to remove Johnson from office by one vote.

In the Watergate hearings, the House was determined to avoid the ugliness of the Johnson impeachment. "Most Americans," said Beschloss, "believe that Nixon's offenses were amply proved and easily of the magnitude to demand his removal."

Getting to that point was not a given—but it is a guide.

THE JUDICIARY COMMITTEE DURING WATERGATE

We were rigorous and resolute on the House Judiciary Committee during Watergate. The framers of the Constitution believed that citizens and their representatives must step forward to protect the country if a chief executive refused to follow the law or drove a stake into the heart of our system. Our committee viewed the process as a way to preserve our freedom.

Our first vote on an impeachment resolution took place on July 27, 1974, after seven months of preparation. A typically steamy day in Washington, the air-conditioned hearing room had heat of a different sort. The space was crammed. Dozens of photographers crouched on the blue carpet, aiming at the two rows set aside for committee members. The room fell silent when the clerk began the roll call. Suddenly I heard my name. I felt jarred; at first, no word would come out. Then I heard myself say, "Yes."

I never realized how hard it would be to vote for the impeachment of a president. It wasn't as though I had any qualms; I had none. I had delved deeply into each issue and felt certain that impeachment was warranted. Although I was a liberal Democrat and Nixon was a conservative Republican, he was still my president. I did not want to see my president abuse power and commit crimes. I did not want to have to vote for impeachment.

And I was not alone. None of the members who voted for impeachment—Democrat or Republican—took any pleasure in doing so. In fact, the chair of the Committee, Peter W. Rodino Jr. of New Jersey, went back to his office afterward and cried. For me, it was one of the most unpleasant and sobering things I ever had to do.

My involvement in the impeachment of Richard Nixon was an accident. In November 1972, I was elected for the first time to the House of Representatives from Brooklyn's 16th Congressional District. When the Watergate break-in took place in June earlier that year, it barely brushed my consciousness. I was fully absorbed in winning my June primary, and, coincidentally, that month, we had to contend with our own break-in at our campaign headquarters. Intruders burst in, roughed up my campaign manager, and took off before we knew what happened. After that, I had a narrow primary victory and immediately had to stave off a series of legal challenges by my opponent, Rep. Emanuel Celler, a fifty-year incumbent, who was supported by the powerful Brooklyn Democratic political machine.

In the November election, Richard Nixon was reelected with one of the largest electoral margins in the country's history. He won forty-nine of fifty states. Most people did not seriously entertain the notion that he was involved in the break-in. Impeachment was not on the map.

I ended up on the Judiciary Committee after House leaders realized I had a law background. At the age of thirty-one, I became one of the youngest committee members. My defeat of Rep, Celler had an unanticipated effect. Celler had been the Judiciary Committee chair, but now the slot went to the quiet and reserved Rodino. Author Jimmy Breslin later said that had Celler—elderly and highly partisan—remained as chair, impeachment never might have happened.

THE WATERGATE EVENTS

Shortly after I started my first term in January 1973, developments began to link the White House to the Watergate burglary and cover-up.

Even for Americans who lived through that era, all but a few unforgettable incidents are distant and blurred. For better or worse, the events that the Judiciary Committee reviewed again and again—a huge catalog of illegal deeds by the president—are still vivid to me. A staff of one hundred (including Hillary Rodham) gathered information. We had thirty-six volumes of evidence with 7,200 pages of information. Some incidents occurred before or were unconnected to the Watergate burglary; others related to the burglary; and yet others came as the president and his cohorts tried to cover tracks.

Context helps in understanding Watergate. The events arose during a time of great political intensity. *Roe* v. *Wade* was decided on January 22, 1973; civil rights, equal opportunity, environmental issues were percolating. The ongoing conflict in Vietnam fueled tensions across the nation. Ending the war was a key impetus to my running for Congress; many people were fervent about peace.

The war was not unrelated to Watergate. The first events on the "Watergate" timetable stretched back to Nixon's attempts to hide his secret and illegal bombing of Cambodia, which began within two months after he first took office in 1969. After an article appeared in the *New York Times* in the spring of 1969 and reporter William Beecher revealed the bombings by the U.S. Air Force, Nixon ordered the FBI to wiretap the telephones of journalists, such as columnist Joseph Kraft, and of his own National Security Council staff. The president's emissary, Alexander Haig, told the FBI not to maintain regular records of the wiretaps.

Ongoing illegal wiretaps continued from 1969 to 1971. Even the president's brother, Donald Nixon, was wiretapped at the president's direction. In July 1970, the president approved the "Huston plan" to conduct electronic surveillance of dissident groups and individuals in the United States, along with break-ins to the homes of U.S. citizens and the illegal opening of their mail. These abuses became evidence for Article II of the impeachment. The president also demanded income tax audits of political critics and copies of tax files of others. These, too, became part of the "Watergate" litany.

In addition, nine months prior to the Watergate break-in, the president authorized a secret unit within the White House, known as "the Plumbers," to conduct a different burglary—that of the office of Daniel Ellsberg's psychiatrist. They carried it out on September 3, 1971. Ellsberg, once a Defense Department employee, had released the secret and explosive Pentagon Papers, the government's own account of massive lies about the Vietnam War. Portions were published in the *New York Times* and *Washington Post*. Nixon, enraged, dispatched his aides to get information to discredit Ellsberg.

Interestingly, Nixon invented a false justification for the burglary of the psychiatrist's office based on "national security" needs. Later, John Ehrlichman, the president's domestic affairs adviser, testified that the president told him: "The break-in was in furtherance of national security and fully justified under the circumstances."

Nixon operated what historian Arthur M. Schlesinger Jr. described as an "imperial presidency." The White House ran without restraint, doing what it wanted, paying no regard to Congress, the Constitution, and the laws. When Nixon disagreed with the monies allocated by Congress for public expenditures, such as for health programs, he simply refused to follow the law and came up with a scheme of "impoundment"—withholding the money from the purposes for which it was intended. He decided on his own to dismantle a federal agency, the Office of Economic Opportunity.

The name of Watergate didn't attach to the abuse and misuse of presidential power until the burglary of the Democratic National Committee headquarters, which were located in the Watergate office complex in D.C. The trail from there eventually led to 1600 Pennsylvania Avenue.

The Watergate burglars were busy planting illegal wiretaps on June 17, 1972, when an ordinary security guard discovered the gang of five men. Wiretaps they had installed in an earlier break-in had glitches, so it was a return trip. At a preliminary hearing the next day, the court found that one burglar, James W. McCord Jr., was a former CIA agent who worked for the Committee to Re-Elect the President. After the arrests, a check for $25,000 intended for the president's reelection committee found its way into the bank account of one of the burglars.

Questions about the connection between the burglars and Nixon's reelection committee arose in the fall, but congressional inquiries were squelched. Public concern grew after the burglars appeared before Judge John J. Sirica on January 8, 1973. Sirica, a conservative Republican judge in Washington, D.C., suspected greater wrongdoing and imposed heavy thirty-year sentences, suggesting leniency might be available if the burglars cooperated with investigators. Sure enough, McCord talked, and pointed the finger to higher-ups in the White House.

As a result, Archibald Cox, an eminent Harvard Law School professor, was appointed as a special prosecutor to investigate Watergate. The U.S. Senate created a Watergate committee, and televised hearings conducted by the redoubtable Senator Sam Ervin of North Carolina, folksy and lawyerly, took center stage in every living room. At those hearings, Howard Baker, a Republican Senator from Tennessee, coined the soon-to-be-famous phrase: "What did the president know and when did he know it?"

That spring, White House counsel John Dean appeared before the committee. He described a startling scene. He revealed that he had told President Nixon of a cover-up of the

Watergate burglary, including payments of hush money and offers of pardons to the burglars. He described it to Nixon as "a cancer" on the presidency. Dean reported that the president, instead of trying to stop the cover-up, suggested a way to get money for payoffs.

Of course, President Nixon disputed Dean's testimony. If true, it would show that the president committed obstruction of justice, a crime. So it was of extreme interest to the Senate committee to hear later from Alexander Butterfield, deputy assistant to the president, of an in-house recording system that taped all of the president's conversations. Tapes could prove whether Dean was telling the truth—and the president was engaged in obstruction of justice—or whether Dean had committed perjury.

The tapes became crucial. Special Prosecutor Cox insisted that they be delivered to him as evidence. The White House objected, but a federal appeals court upheld Cox's right to have the tapes. And this triggered the "Saturday Night Massacre" on October 20, 1973. President Nixon ordered Cox to drop his request for the tapes; Cox refused. The president then ordered the attorney general to fire him. But Attorney General Elliot Richardson and his Deputy Attorney General Bill Ruckelshaus resigned in protest rather than fire Cox. Solicitor General Robert Bork, left by virtue of the resignations as the highest official at the Justice Department, complied and fired Cox.

The events set off a firestorm of public outrage. The American people flooded Congress with phone calls and telegrams.

No president was going to stop a criminal investigation. Something had to be done.

This was the turning point for me, too. I had been back in my home district in Brooklyn, and heard the news. I couldn't believe it. Where would it end? The rule of law meant no one was above the law. Returning to Washington, I was intent on seeing an impeachment inquiry begin. So were others.

INVESTIGATION AND INQUIRY

After the Saturday Night Massacre, the public fury could not be ignored.

Under the Constitution, the House of Representatives is responsible for initiating the presidential impeachment process. Although controlled by the Democrats during Watergate, the House of Representatives had been in no hurry to start impeachment proceedings. Perhaps the bad memory of the partisan Andrew Johnson impeachment in the 1800s was a factor. Perhaps the natural inertia of the government played a role. And possibly Nixon's landslide victory less than a year earlier had an impact.

In any case, that reluctance was right. The act of impeachment should never be undertaken lightly, or without overwhelming cause. Impeachment is a constitutional last resort.

The House leadership's reluctance to move forward had been obvious that summer when Father Robert Drinan, a representative from Massachusetts, introduced an impeachment resolution on July 31, 1973. Simply stated, it went nowhere.

A member of the House Judiciary Committee and a former law school dean, Father Drinan made the introduction after revelations that Nixon had ordered the secret bombing of Cambodia, a neutral country. This massive bombing campaign was concealed and recorded in a secret set of military logs that, on orders from Nixon, were hidden from Congress and the public. Congress had never authorized funding for military activity in Cambodia, unlike the support it gave for the Vietnam War. Father Drinan wanted to hold President Nixon accountable, but the House did nothing to support him.

Now, however, the House leadership took action and instructed the Judiciary Committee to begin an impeachment inquiry. On February 6, 1974, the full House approved Resolution 803, a Resolution of Inquiry "to investigate fully and completely whether sufficient grounds exist for the House of Representatives to exercise its constitutional power to impeach Richard M. Nixon."

The resolution gave the Judiciary Committee subpoena power to require testimony or the production of documents, including memos, correspondence, and tape recordings; the power to hold hearings; and the funds needed to carry out the investigation.

Using the House Judiciary Committee instead of a newly formed "special committee" of handpicked legislators prevented charges that the deck was stacked. The decision showed the seriousness of the House leadership on impeachment: they didn't know what the outcome would be, but they wanted to avoid missteps along the way.

Congressman Rodino also displayed astuteness in hiring John Doar, a Republican. As impeachment counsel, Doar would collect the evidence and present the case to the Committee. By picking a Republican as top committee staff, Rodino signaled that he understood impeachment needed to be bipartisan.

Once the impeachment inquiry formally opened, the spotlight turned to the Judiciary Committee. First of all, we had to understand what the Constitution said. I remember taking out my pocket version to look up the relevant provision:

> Article II, Section 4: *The President, Vice-President and all Civil Officers of the United States, shall be removed from Office on Impeachment for, and Conviction of, Treason, Bribery, or other high Crimes and Misdemeanors.*

Neither treason nor bribery, two of the bases for presidential impeachment, seemed present here. That left "other high Crimes and Misdemeanors." What did that phrase mean? In three years of law school at Harvard, we never touched upon impeachment. I suspect my colleagues, all lawyers, never had encountered the subject either. We were on our own.

I searched dusty library tomes of ancient English law, looking for clues to understanding the founders' language. A new scholarly work by a Harvard professor Raoul Berger offered guidance, and the Committee staff wrote a memo, trying to define the term "high crimes and misdemeanors." (See Chapter Two.)

The Nixon White House, to make impeachment more difficult, contended that impeachment was available only if the president were shown to have committed an actual crime. But history indicated that the founders had something much different and broader in mind, related to subversion of the Constitution and abuse of power (see Chapter Two). The Committee debated the issue, and a bipartisan majority agreed that the term meant "grave abuses of government power," not necessarily a criminal act.

Doar and the committee staff interviewed witnesses, collected documents, and gathered evidence. The information was crammed into big black notebooks that we had to keep locked in our safes, away from prying eyes. Each statement of evidence was contained on a single page, followed by the backup documentation that supported it. In April, Doar subpoenaed copies of tapes from the White House, including the Dean conversation, so that the committee could discern what knowledge the president had and what actions he took. The president balked at delivering all of the tapes, as he had before. The Supreme Court ultimately ordered that they be delivered to a grand jury, but we didn't have them before our vote on impeachment resolutions.

To make sure the Committee members understood the evidence, Doar and his staff went over each allegation in detail, even reading them aloud to us. We could then challenge the statement, question the sources, and probe the evidence in order to satisfy ourselves that the statement was accurate.

All in all, the process was exhaustive and exhausting. But, by design, it was as fair as possible. President Nixon was represented by counsel, who could call witnesses on his behalf, cross-examine our witnesses, file briefs, and argue his position to us fully and completely.

After some internal back-and-forth, the committee also decided to allow the hearings to be televised. This turned out to be critical for public support. The American people could hear the members of the Committee discuss and debate the facts and the Constitution, and they could look at our faces and weigh our words and determine whether we were being sincere, thoughtful, and responsible.

"The committee had impressed those who watched its deliberations . . . with its competence and evenhandedness," wrote *New York Times* reporter R. W. Apple, Jr. No one at any point could—or did—argue seriously that the proceedings were biased.

ARTICLES OF IMPEACHMENT TAKE SHAPE

The Judiciary Committee adopted three articles of impeachment. It rejected two others. The articles began:

> *RESOLVED, That Richard M. Nixon, President of the United States, is impeached for high crimes and misdemeanors.*
>
> (See Appendix E.)

Each Article of Impeachment contained an overview of the charge followed by specific instances of conduct by the president that constituted the charge. Through this formulation, the many illegal activities of the president were grouped into large categories, followed by reams of detail and backup information.

Article I began:

> *In his conduct of the office of President of the United States, Richard M. Nixon, in violation of his constitutional oath faithfully to execute the office of President of United States and, to the best of his ability, preserve, protect, and defend the Constitution of the United States, and in violation of his constitutional duty to take care that the laws be faithfully executed. . . .*

This first article focused on obstruction of justice and dealt with the cover-up of the Watergate burglary. It addressed issues of a quasi-criminal nature. The president, it said, "has prevented, obstructed, and impeded the administration of justice."

The Committee laid out the president's efforts to provide hush money and offer presidential pardons to keep the burglars from implicating higher-ups. Also specified were the president's actions in making false or misleading statements to government investigators, counseling others to give false or misleading testimony, and withholding material evidence. It detailed the president's conversations with the head of the Justice Department's Criminal Division, in which Nixon asked for secret information about what witnesses were telling the grand jury and then used that information to have other witnesses coached.

In Article I, the president also was accused of secretly inducing people to lie under oath, in a series of allegations of suborning perjury. Nixon told his aide, Bob Haldeman, for example, to tell the Senate committee that the president had rejected hush money, when he had not; Haldeman followed the instructions and was ultimately indicted, convicted, and sentenced to jail for perjury.

Article I concluded:

> *Richard M. Nixon has acted in a manner contrary to his trust as President and subversive of constitutional government, to the great prejudice of the cause of law and justice and to the manifest injury to the people of the United States.*

The vote in favor of this article was 27 to 11, including all the Democrats and 6 of the 17 Republicans.

The second article of impeachment rested on the concept that removal is warranted when a president abuses the powers of his office so seriously that his actions jeopardize the rights of Americans or subvert the operations of the government.

The use of warrantless wiretaps by President Nixon fell among the abuses in this category. So did the so-called "enemies list," by which President Nixon ordered IRS audits of people who opposed his policies on the Vietnam War.

Also listed in this article of impeachment was the president's failure to correct or stop false testimony to Congress. For example, Richard Kleindienst, a candidate for attorney general, testified to Congress that no one had interfered with the handling of an antitrust suit in the Department of Justice. He was lying and the president (who had ordered the interference) knew it.

There were many other grounds cited as abuses of power, and some of the instances in which the president misused his office were astonishing. I remember my first reaction to listening to the presidential tape recordings—people in the Oval Office sounded like petty criminals cooking up some plot. I never once heard the president talk about what was the right thing to do or what was in the best interests of our country. Instead, the entire focus of the conversation was how to avoid criminal charges and how to beat out investigations.

The evidence for impeachment was overwhelming.

Of all the articles of impeachment, abuse of powers won the most support from Republicans, and, as a result, had the largest vote in the committee—28 in favor, 10 against—although I found it strange that anyone could vote against it. All of the Democrats and 7 Republicans supported it.

The Committee, again with a bipartisan vote, also adopted a third article of impeachment. This was for the president's stonewalling the impeachment inquiry.

Article III stated that the President "has failed without lawful cause or excuse to produce papers and things as directed by duly authorized subpoenas issued by the Committee on the Judiciary of the House of Representatives."

President Nixon had refused to comply with Committee subpoenas seeking presidential tape recordings and documents. Nixon treated our inquiry with arrogance and contempt. He had provided the Committee with false transcripts of tape recordings in an effort to minimize his role in obstruction of justice and abuses of power. While proclaiming to the public that he was fully cooperating with us, in reality, he was not.

The legal theory behind Article III held that the president's obstruction of an impeachment inquiry undermined and attacked our system of checks and balances. We found this activity contrary to the trust placed in the president "and subversive of constitutional government, to the great prejudice of the cause of law and justice, and to the manifest injury of the people of the United States."

The vote on this was 21 to 17.

Two other Articles of Impeachment were introduced, but not adopted. One had to do with the president's use of improper tax deductions and his personal enrichment from the expenditure of government funds on his private properties. The article failed because the matters, although wrong, did not pose a threat to democracy.

The other article that failed had to do with the president's concealment of his illegal bombing campaign in Cambodia. I felt so strongly about the Cambodia bombing that I drafted the resolution of impeachment to hold him accountable, and asked Rep. John Conyers, Jr., who had more seniority, to introduce it. (See Appendix F.) Ultimately, the committee didn't approve it (See Chapter Three.) But as I looked closely at all of President Nixon's illegal activities, I believed that the bombing of Cambodia had formed the impetus for much of his other arrogant corruption of power. He had, after all, begun illegal wiretapping in 1969 to prevent information about the secret bombing from reaching the public. It seemed to me to be a root cause of much of his illegal and abusive activity.

THE PRESIDENT RESIGNS

I voted for all five impeachment resolutions, although today I might view the article on tax deductions, standing alone, as insufficient.

The three resolutions that passed had substantial Republican support, and, more important, public support.

Support for impeachment actually grew after the Committee's vote, when President Nixon had to produce tapes that had been subpoenaed by the grand jury. The Supreme Court, including justices appointed by Nixon, ruled unanimously against him. On one tape—from the day after the Watergate break-in—President Nixon is heard ordering his chief of staff to get the CIA to stop the FBI's investigation into the burglary by claiming national security issues would be compromised. The president was really trying to conceal a trail that might lead to him. Once the holdout Republicans on the Committee saw the transcript, they joined with the rest of us and agreed that the president should be impeached. Now, every representative on the House Judiciary Committee stood in favor of impeachment.

Next, the full House of Representatives would vote on impeachment and, if passed, they would be referred to the Senate for trial. With the release of the tapes and the switch of Republican holdouts, the House would have voted over-whelmingly for impeachment and the Senate would have voted overwhelmingly for Nixon's removal from office. When Republicans leaders delivered this news to President Nixon, he opted to resign.

SHARP TURN ON CLINTON

Although the Nixon impeachment involved remedying an abuse of presidential powers, I saw the Clinton impeachment as an abuse of congressional powers.

For me it was particularly sad. The House Judiciary Com-mittee turned away from its proud history. In the Nixon era, the Committee helped restore the nation's constitutional health after grave presidential abuses. Now, the Committee was consumed with partisanship—acting without constitu-tional basis and destroying the reputation it had acquired for judicious handling of the Nixon impeachment.

Everything about the Clinton impeachment tells a vastly different story from what we witnessed in Nixon's case. The nature of the charges, the process, and the history leading up to it are a study in contrasts.

Clinton's ordeal began with a newspaper story that ques-tioned whether the president had been involved in a shaky, and possibly criminal, land deal in Arkansas prior to becoming pres-ident. The facts of this Whitewater scandal were extraordinarily complex. The Republicans insisted on an investigation.

Under the Independent Counsel Act that I had helped author in 1978, a special three-judge panel appoints a special prosecutor when serious allegations are raised against the president. The panel decided to appoint Kenneth Starr, a Washington lawyer with no prosecutorial experience, but very close ties to the extreme right wing of the Republican Party. Starr had even briefly represented a woman who had brought a lawsuit against President Clinton, a fact that should have precluded him from serving because it gave the appearance of bias.

From the time I read about it, the Starr selection worried me. Would Starr put his right-wing connections aside and handle the matter with neutrality and good judgment? Or would he use the power of his position to score partisan points?

Even though he spent millions of dollars digging into the Whitewater matter, Starr never found criminal wrongdoing by President Clinton in the Arkansas land deals. What his investigation did produce, however, was the recommendation that Congress undertake an impeachment inquiry—not into Whitewater—but into President Clinton's sexual involvement with a twenty-something White House intern, and later government employee, Monica Lewinsky.

How did Starr get from an Arkansas land deal to oral sex in the Oval Office?

After receiving information from a woman who had befriended Lewinsky, Starr asked Attorney General Reno to expand his investigation. Starr claimed Clinton—in a private lawsuit brought against him by another woman—manipulated Lewinsky to prevent her from disclosing their encounters. Starr wanted to investigate this as an obstruction of justice. I thought that if the attorney general believed there were a serious issue to investigate, she should have sought the appointment of a different independent counsel. But Starr was permitted to carry his land deal investigation into this claim.

Starr, an obviously prudish man, was horrified at Clinton's sexual dalliance and produced a lengthy and highly salacious report, recounting it in detail. The report said that the president had made false statements in legal proceedings about his relationship with Lewinsky, and denied the relationship to the public. For these acts, Starr said, the president should be impeached for high crimes and misdemeanors. The report was delivered to the House Judiciary Committee, which immediately turned around and released it to the public and began hearings of a highly partisan nature.

I couldn't believe what had happened. Starr himself never should have issued a recommendation on impeachment; as the author of the special prosecutor statute, I believed that he had no authority to do so. His role was to investigate allegations of criminal conduct by persons in the highest offices. If criminal acts were involved, he could have prosecuted them, as is happening in the Bush administration with the investigation by Special Prosecutor Patrick Fitzgerald into the outing of a covert CIA agent by White House staff. The special prosecutor law was never intended to create a grand inquisitor for impeachment. The impetus for impeachment, I always believed, had to come from the public or from the Congress itself.

Just as bad was the reaction of the House Judiciary Committee. The report should have been carefully reviewed by the

Committee before any action was taken upon it. Instead, the Committee released it publicly, hoping to generate adverse public reaction toward President Clinton. In Watergate, we would not have issued a report without giving the president a chance to be heard. And we never would have released a document like the one Starr wrote—a dossier of loaded language and allegations.

The overzealousness of that report ultimately discredited Starr and the impeachment effort. From the outset, it seemed highly partisan. The public was disgusted by the unnecessary sexual content. Polls reported that the people didn't believe that the president's conduct warranted impeachment: having and concealing oral sex with an intern, while certainly not laudable behavior, did not represent the threat to democracy that impeachment was designed to address. The public responded with common sense.

But that didn't stop the Republicans on the House Judiciary Committee from deciding to hold an inquiry into impeachment anyhow. The Democrats opposed it.

The White House asked me to appear before the House Judiciary Committee to explain the standards we used in Nixon's impeachment. I spoke to the House Committee on behalf of the president in early December 1998 with two colleagues from the Watergate hearings: Father Robert Drinan and former Representative Wayne Owens. In this good company, I tried to point out that impeachment was designed to address an abuse of power and to remove a president whose abuses constituted a threat to our democracy. Neither Starr's report nor anything else in the case against President Clinton showed abuse of power affecting our democratic system.

I addressed the Committee about the importance of acting on a bipartisan basis. In Watergate, I noted, the American people called on the Congress to act, not the other way around. Impeachment, I reiterated, as a tool to remove a president from office, is a last resort to preserve democracy. It should not—must not, I said—be trivialized.

My arguments—and similar ones by others—made no dent in the rigid stance of Republican Committee members.

The whole sorry incident of impeaching Clinton was the "political equivalent of nuclear escalation," said Peter Baker in his book, *The Breach.* "For all of the titillation about thongs and cigars, the story of the impeachment and trial of William Jefferson Clinton was not so much about sex as it was about power," he wrote. "The clearest lesson from Watergate was that impeachment had to be bipartisan to work, and yet [in the case of Clinton] the GOP majority pushed forward with little serious effort to win over Democrats."

The outcome was predictable. After the House voted entirely on party lines to impeach President Clinton on two articles—perjury and obstruction of justice—the matter failed to win over the Senate, also on party lines. Not one Democrat in the Senate supported the impeachment. As a result, after an eighteen-day trial, the Republican majority failed to obtain the two-thirds of the Senate needed to remove President Clinton from office. A partisan impeachment, not grounded in serious abuses of power and opposed by the American people, was destined to fail.

Congressional overreaching in the Clinton case should not make us shy away from acting now to stop grave abuses to our constitutional system by President Bush.

OUR SHARED VALUES

At the moment that President Nixon left office, I felt relieved. I thought the long nightmare of presidential criminality and abuses of power was finally over. Rather than weaken the country, as some predicted, the Nixon impeachment strengthened us.

True, the president failed us. But the other institutions of our government did not. A Republican federal judge, John J. Sirica, did the right thing; the Supreme Court, with two Nixon appointees, unanimously rejected Nixon's claim of executive privilege to withhold information and required him to deliver tapes to the grand jury; and the Congress won the respect of the entire nation.

We also discovered basic shared values as Americans—that more important than any single president was the survival of our democracy and our constitutional system itself.

If our constitutional system is to remain robust in the face of brash threats and overarching abuses of power, we need to reclaim those shared values once again. Fortunately, the framers of the Constitution used their experiences with tyranny and their wisdom about the hallmarks of freedom to provide a remedy to preserve our values—impeachment.

CHAPTER TWO

How Impeachment Works

THE CONCEPT OF IMPEACHMENT

Impeachment is as an essential tool for preserving democracy.

Determined to provide protections against grave abuses of power by a president, the framers of the U.S. Constitution created the impeachment process as a special procedure for citizens, through their representatives, to remove a president run amok.

Our founders knew all too well the problems of abuse of power, having thrown off a king who used his unlimited powers oppressively against the colonists. They created a new form of government that was designed to preserve liberty by breaking up power among three co-equal branches of government and instituting a system of checks and balances.

But they worried deeply about presidential misconduct. Left unchallenged, it could be "fatal to the Republic," said James Madison. The new democracy needed the ability to remove a president, if necessary.

Impeachment was the solution. Article II, Section 4 of the Constitution states that a president may be removed for "Treason, Bribery or other high Crimes and Misdemeanors." The Constitution authorizes the same procedure for the vice president and civil officers. (See Appendix A (i).)

THE PROCESS OF IMPEACHMENT

Impeachment is the first step of a two-stage process that can result in the removal of a president from office. The House of Representatives first decides whether to charge the president with impeachable offenses. A majority of the House must vote to impeach.

In Nixon's case, the House Judiciary Committee was asked to conduct an investigation into impeachment and make recommendations before the full House voted. If the full House votes to impeach, articles of impeachment, which contain the charges, are forwarded to the Senate. Stage two is the trial. The chief justice of the Supreme Court presides over a trial in the Senate, and if two-thirds of the senators vote for conviction on the articles of impeachment, the president is removed from office.

Supreme Court Justice Joseph Story, one of the great commentators on the Constitution, said the main thrust of impeachment is not to punish the officeholder but to "secure the state against gross official misdemeanors. It touches neither his person, nor his property, but simply divests him of his political capacity."

GROUNDS FOR IMPEACHMENT

The grounds for removal of a president are stated in the Constitution in a phrase of only eight words: "treason, bribery, or other high crimes and misdemeanors."

Understanding the meaning of this spare language is helped by looking at the original debates on the Constitution.

In adopting the impeachment provision, the framers readily identified treason and bribery as two key reasons for the removal of a president. Treason is defined in the Constitution as providing "aid and comfort" to enemies or "levying war" against the United States. Bribery is a well-established concept that hasn't changed much over the centuries. These two grounds would permit the removal of a president who was threatening the safety of the country or the integrity of government operations.

But the framers believed that these grounds were not sufficient. A president should also be removed for other "great and dangerous offenses" or "attempts to subvert the Constitution," in the words of George Mason, a delegate from Virginia to the Constitutional Convention. (See Appendix A (ii).)

The grounds were expanded to include "high crimes and misdemeanors." To the modern ear, the term seems to suggest a particularly bad kind of criminal conduct. But its actual meaning is different.

"High crimes and misdemeanors" is an archaic phrase that the framers borrowed from British terminology dating back to the fourteenth century. It was defined as "an injury to the state or system of government." As Harvard scholar Raoul Berger noted, the term in Britain covered corruption, misapplication of funds, abuse of official power, neglect of duty, and actions interfering with Parliamentary prerogatives.

Alexander Hamilton explained in Federalist Paper Number 65 that impeachment reached "those offences which proceed from the misconduct of public men or, in other words, from the abuse or violation of some public trust. They are of a nature which may . . . be denominated POLITICAL, as they relate chiefly to injuries done immediately to the society itself."

In essence, the phrase "high crimes and misdemeanors" describes a political crime, a serious and grave abuse of power or an abuse of public trust.

The Constitution doesn't spell out each and every kind of misconduct that qualifies as an impeachable offense, just as it doesn't spell out the details of Congress's right to regulate interstate commerce. Airplanes weren't foreseen in 1789 and neither was wiretapping. But that doesn't prevent Congress from regulating air traffic safety, nor does it prevent impeachment for wiretapping in violation of a federal statute.

While not precise, the term high "crimes and misdemeanors" is sufficient to protect our democracy from a runaway president.

THE IMPEACHABLE OFFENSE DOES NOT HAVE TO BE A CRIME

High crimes and misdemeanors are not limited to actual crimes. We debated this in the Judiciary Committee during

Watergate and reached a firm conclusion on this topic. While commission of a crime may be grounds for impeachment, the phrase also covers conduct that is not a violation of the criminal code.

The key is whether the conduct is a grave abuse of power or subversion of the Constitution. Some presidential misdeeds we encountered in the Nixon impeachment had a basis in the criminal law; others did not. (Nixon, after he resigned, was given a pardon by President Gerald Ford, a matter of deep controversy at the time but one that immunized him from criminal prosecution.)

In this regard, the first article of impeachment against Nixon encompassed obstructing justice and inducing perjury—also crimes. But the second article was framed in terms of abuse of power without reference to the criminal code. President Nixon's creation of an "enemies list" of political critics to be audited by the IRS was viewed as a high crime and misdemeanor. The use of government powers to harass political opponents and the subversion of tax enforcement into a tool of political oppression were political crimes but not criminal code violations.

On the flip side, not all violations of the criminal code are political crimes that necessarily rise to the standard of high crimes and misdemeanors. In President Nixon's case, the House Judiciary Committee declined to adopt an impeachment resolution on grounds relating to Nixon's improper use of a tax deduction, a bad deed but not subversion of democracy.

THE STANDARD OF PRESIDENTIAL
RESPONSIBILITY AND IMPEACHMENT

An analysis of history and the founders' writings leaves open the question of whether a president may be impeached for the misdeeds of subordinates.

During the Nixon impeachment process, the House Judiciary Committee decided to take a conservative approach. We limited impeachable offenses to misdeeds in which the president had personal responsibility—through participation in misconduct, or authorization or ratification of it. The president's personal knowledge and personal actions were key.

This standard, while high, is also the right approach. A president should not be impeached for all of the "bad things" that take place during the term of office. But, on the other hand, a president must be held accountable for grave abuses of power in which he participated.

When an action is taken by a subordinate, but is directed by the president, the president bears personal responsibility. When the action by a subordinate is unknown to the president, but he later endorses or condones it, or attempts to cover it up, the president is personally responsible. The president is also responsible if he turns a blind eye to serious misdeeds of which he is notified. But if a subordinate engages in misconduct without the president's participation, knowledge, authorization or acceptance, a standard for impeachment may not be met.

Impeachment is also justifiable for matters that did not arise in Nixon's case—a president's failure to accept his responsibility to act when the lives of many Americans are threatened.

The central questions in Watergate are still relevant: What did the president know? When did he know it? And in the case of President Bush, there is a third question: Once provided with the knowledge, what did he do about it?

PRESIDENTIAL OBLIGATIONS AND IMPEACHMENT

Under the Constitution, the president has three central obligations. (See Appendix B.)

First, the president must "faithfully execute the Office of President of the United States." This is part of the oath of office, which is itself mandated by the Constitution.

Second, the president must "preserve, protect, and defend the Constitution of the United States," also part of the oath of office. In other words, the president is required to respect the role of the Congress and the courts, as well as the fundamental liberties reserved to the citizens.

And third, the president is required "to take Care that the Laws be faithfully executed," an affirmative duty imposed directly by the Constitution. This presidential obligation is one of the most important. Involved are two responsibilities, similar but separate: first, the president is required to "take care," or to be highly attentive, and, second, the president must see that the laws are "faithfully executed" or that the laws are fully followed. Combined, these impose a very strict burden on the president to ensure the proper implementation of the nation's laws.

A president cannot be impeached lightly. The framers rejected the notion of presidential impeachment for "maladministration." The term was, at one point, inserted in the impeachment provision but then replaced by "high crimes and misdemeanors." The framers thought maladministration was too vague and worried that it might put the president at the mercy of an overreaching Congress.

What *is* expected is that the president will uphold the Constitution and the laws and fulfill the oath of office. Carefully applying the law is a requirement for holding office. The president may not avoid, subvert, or undermine the law.

Nothing excuses the president from fulfilling his constitutional obligations—not incompetence or ignorance or lack of interest. The failure or the inability of a president to fulfill these obligations, for whatever reason, causes serious harm to democracy. Impeachment is the constitutional remedy to protect the health of the nation.

A SUMMARY OF IMPEACHABLE OFFENSES OF PRESIDENT GEORGE W. BUSH

President Bush has engaged in acts that violate his obligations as president on a range of issues:

These impeachable offenses include

- The president deceived Congress and the people in taking the country to war in Iraq.
- The president directed an illegal domestic wiretapping program and other surveillance of Americans.
- The president permitted and condoned the use of torture or cruel treatment of detainees.

- The president showed reckless indifference to human life in the face of Hurricane Katrina and in equipping U.S. soldiers and planning for the occupation of Iraq.
- The president tried to cover up his war deceptions with the leak of misleading classified information, an act that became entangled with the outing of a CIA agent, a possible crime.

IMPEACHABLE OFFENSES OF GEORGE W. BUSH FOR DECEPTIONS IN TAKING THE COUNTRY INTO WAR IN IRAQ

War, in the view of the framers of the Constitution, would create one of the greatest temptations of a president to abuse power. Edmund Randolph, a member of the Constitutional Convention, noted, "The Executive will have great opportunities of abusing his power; particularly in time of war when the military force, and in some respects the public money, will be in his hands."

One of the grounds for the impeachment of President Bush addresses his deceptions and misrepresentations in leading the country to war in Iraq.

Although no president has been impeached for misuse of war powers, an article of impeachment was proposed against President Nixon for his secret bombing of Cambodia.

Under the Constitution, Congress has at least an equal say with the president about war making through its powers to declare and fund war. The president is made the "commander in chief" who directs the army and navy.

The president used false premises to drive the country to war, insisting that Iraq was developing nuclear weapons of mass destruction and linking Saddam Hussein to al Qaeda and 9/11. The consequences have been enormous, and there is no endpoint in duration or lives lost in Iraq.

Taking our country into war based on false information is an arrogation of presidential war making power. Deceit nullifies the right and obligation of Congress to understand the issues at stake and to decide whether to support the war. The right of the American people to participate in the decision is cast aside. The actions "subvert the Constitution" under founder George Mason's definition of impeachable offenses.

James Iredell, a justice on the first Supreme Court and noted participant in the North Carolina ratification debates on the Constitution, commented about impeachment that "the President must certainly be punishable for giving false information to the Senate." In responding to a complaint that the Senate would be too cozy with the president to vote for impeachment, Iredell disagreed, insisting that the Senate would not react kindly if a president "concealed important intelligence which he ought to have communicated, and by that means induced them to enter into measures injurious to their country."

Unless a clear message is sent, there is no way to ensure that the use of deceptions to lead the country to war will not be repeated by this president or another. There is no remedy other than impeachment to protect the United States now and in the future from an act so egregious. (See Chapter Three.)

IMPEACHABLE OFFENSES OF GEORGE W. BUSH FOR VIOLATING THE LAW ON WIRETAPPING

Violation of the law is clearly a basis for impeachment, especially when the acts involve an abuse of power or subvert democracy.

In Nixon's case, the House Judiciary Committee listed numerous violations of the law; one article of impeachment alone included more than two dozen instances of obstruction of justice.

When a president deliberately refuses to abide by the law, impeachment is a proper remedy. President Bush admitted that he has not complied with the Foreign Intelligence Surveillance Act of 1978 and is engaging in domestic surveillance without seeking court orders. He said he plans to continue this conduct, even though his actions may invade the privacy and constitutional rights of thousands upon thousands of Americans.

The president's refusal to obey the statute, which carries a criminal penalty, violates his duty to take care that the laws are faithfully executed. It contravenes his oath of office, which requires him to obey the laws, and preserve, protect, and defend the Constitution.

Over the years, the president has publicly misrepresented the wiretapping programs, stating that no surveillance was being undertaken without a court order. President Nixon's repeated lying to the American public formed the basis of one of the grounds for impeachment against him. President Bush's deceptions may form the grounds for impeachment, as well.

A second secret domestic surveillance program exposed in May 2006 collects and tracks the telephone calls of millions of Americans under the guise of foreign intelligence surveillance. This program, begun without the approval of Congress or the courts, poses many potential violations of the law, and as details are uncovered, further grounds for impeachment also may be identified.

President Bush has improperly attempted to justify his illegal surveillance as falling within his power as commander in chief. The president's failure to recognize that he is bound by a constitutional system in which he is only one of three players and his abuse of his role as commander in chief threaten our democracy to its core, and are grounds for impeachment and removal from office. (See Chapter Four.)

IMPEACHABLE OFFENSES OF GEORGE W. BUSH IN PERMITTING AND CONDONING THE MISTREATMENT OF U.S. DETAINEES

Congress has enacted laws prohibiting the mistreatment or torture of prisoners in U.S. hands. The War Crimes Act of 1996 makes it a crime to violate provisions of the Geneva Conventions that ban torture and cruel or degrading treatment. Ratified by the United States in 1955, the Geneva Conventions are the law of the land, as is the Convention against Torture. The U.S. government has long adhered to the laws and treaties that prevent mistreatment of prisoners.

President Bush unilaterally changed U.S. practice and policy by a memo in 2002, rejecting the application of the Geneva Conventions and enabling U.S. personnel to conduct brutal interrogations without fear of prosecution.

In so doing, the president tried to void a U.S. law and permitted others to avoid it. The president may not violate treaties or interpret them in ways designed to nullify their essential purpose.

The president's refusal to obey the laws prohibiting torture and cruel or inhuman treatment of detainees is an impeachable offense.

In addition, when evidence emerged of abusive treatment in U.S. military detention facilities, the president had an affirmative duty to institute a thorough and full investigation of all persons in the chain of command, from top to bottom. He has not done so. This responsibility is spelled out in the Geneva Conventions. The president is also required to take care that the laws are faithfully executed, including the War Crimes Act and the Anti-Torture Act. President Bush has failed to see that the responsible parties, including higher-ups, are held accountable. These failures are impeachable offenses.

When Congress reaffirmed its opposition to torture and cruel or degrading treatment of detainees in an antitorture statute passed in 2005, the president was disdainful. He added a statement when he signed the bill, indicating he need not be bound by the law. Impeachment is the only way to

prevent a president from continuing to disregard his obligations under the Constitution to enforce the law, not to break
it. (See Chapter Five.)

IMPEACHABLE OFFENSES OF GEORGE W. BUSH FOR RECKLESS INDIFFERENCE TO HUMAN LIFE IN KATRINA AND IRAQ

President Bush has shown a reckless indifference to human
life in failing to marshal emergency resources in response to
Hurricane Katrina. This type of gross negligence is also
apparent in his decision to invade Iraq without providing protective equipment to soldiers and without having an adequate
post-invasion plan.

If the president's actions were simple negligence, they
might not amount to impeachable offenses. In the debates at
the Constitutional Convention of 1787, one of the grounds
initially raised for impeachment was "neglect of duty." The
Committee on Detail changed that language to "treason and
bribery," which was in turn expanded by adding "high crimes
and misdemeanors." (See Appendix A (ii).)

When the framers used the British term "high crimes and
misdemeanors," they were undoubtedly familiar with its history. At least two noteworthy impeachments for neglect
occurred in Britain: one involved the neglect of the commis-
sioner of the navy to prepare adequately against a Dutch
invasion; the other related to neglect by an admiral who failed
to safeguard the seas. In a classic nineteenth-century text on
constitutional interpretation, Judge Thomas M. Cooley of the

Michigan Supreme Court states that impeachment can result from "inexcusable neglects of duty, which are dangerous and criminal because of the immense interests involved and the greatness of the trust which has not been kept."

President Bush's actions in Katrina and Iraq are "inexcusable neglects."

When Hurricane Katrina threatened New Orleans, President Bush was personally informed of an impending catastrophe, but did not take the necessary actions to protect human lives. Under law, he alone was empowered to mobilize additional federal resources. He did not "take care" that the laws were faithfully executed.

In addition, President Bush's failure to provide sufficient body armor and equipment protection for our troops in Iraq or to develop a proper plan for the occupation of Iraq after the invasion are violations of his obligation to "take care." U.S. soldiers and the American people trusted the president to exercise special care in making complete and thorough preparations.

The president neglected his duty over matters of vast consequence and in situations where the trust placed in him was great. This conjunction of the failure to take care and reckless indifference to human life provides the basis for impeachment. (See Chapter Six.)

IMPEACHABLE OFFENSES OF GEORGE W. BUSH FOR LEAKING CLASSIFIED INFORMATION

Several months after the Iraq War started, President Bush authorized I. Lewis "Scooter" Libby, a top White House aide, to leak selected passages of a classified document to key reporters. The leak came in response to criticism that the president had deceived the country about Iraq's nuclear weapons capability in his State of the Union address. The criticism was accurate, but the leak actually distorted the truth.

The leak was intertwined with the "outing" of a covert CIA agent married to the Bush critic.

Declassifying information to mislead the public and cover up presidential deceptions about war making is an abuse of power. If the facts, as yet unknown, show that President Bush had any role in releasing the identity of a covert CIA agent, a potential violation of federal law, that would be an impeachable offense. (See Chapter Seven.)

PUTTING THE CONSTITUTION TO WORK

President Bush has committed a great many grave and dangerous offenses, and subverted the Constitution. The evidence is clear and strong. Congress cannot shirk its responsibility to protect the nation from tyranny. This is what the founders of this country intended when they added presidential impeachment to the Constitution.

CHAPTER THREE

Impeachment for Deceptions in Taking the Country into War in Iraq

OVERVIEW

On the first anniversary of 9/11, the streets of New York City were empty. Many shop owners closed for the day. One by one, the names of the people who died in the World Trade Center attacks were read in a solemn ceremony. Bells rang throughout the city. Elsewhere, people stopped their daily lives to memorialize those who perished.

At a time of national sadness, President Bush and his top administration officials banded together to create urgency for a war in Iraq. Building on still-raw memories of 9/11, this was the week that the White House chose to roll out its "marketing plan" for the war, as the president's chief of staff Andrew Card described those days in September.

Iraq, we were told by one administration official after another, constituted a threat to Americans, and something needed to be done. On one television show, National Security Advisor Condoleezza Rice said the United States might experience the "mushroom cloud" from a nuclear strike by Iraq unless the country acted quickly. On another program, Vice President Dick Cheney announced with "absolute certainty" that Saddam Hussein was buying the equipment to build a nuclear weapon. The president echoed these sentiments in a speech to the United Nations General Assembly on September 12, 2002, declaring that Iraq had nuclear weapons capacity. Two weeks later, he described this capacity as "clear evidence of peril" and a "gathering" threat.

The Bush administration insisted that Iraq had nuclear weapons that could harm the United States and that Saddam Hussein worked with the terrorists who struck the United States on 9/11.

What the Bush administration was selling in this relentless campaign was no ordinary product. It was war. Lives could — and would —be lost; billions could—and would—be spent; consequences could —and would —disastrous. It was the most critical decision that a nation could make.

But there were big problems with the statements being bandied by the president. The claims about Iraq's nuclear threat were untrue. The claims about an Iraqi connection to the September 11 attacks were untrue. The claims about an immediate need to take action against Iraq were untrue.

The president knew these assertions were untrue, or had reason to know they were untrue. And yet, he made them and repeated them. He permitted others in his administration to make them and to repeat them, without the slightest effort at correction.

These acts are high crimes and misdemeanors. These acts are impeachable offenses.

FALSE STATEMENTS DRIVING THE COUNTRY INTO WAR

While the war in Iraq started by President Bush on March 19, 2003, was based on a series of false claims, the real reasons for the invasion remain hidden.

Was it for oil? Was it to avenge his father, who was the target of an assassination attempt allegedly sponsored by Saddam Hussein? Or was it led by superhawks, stung when Bush I rejected their proposals to invade Iraq in the 1991 Persian Gulf War because, he later explained in *Time* magazine, it would incur "incalculable human and political costs." Was it to advance a neoconservative idea to establish new permanent American military bases and the expansion of global interests? Had we embarked on an interventionist foreign policy to install a government more to our liking? Was it to burnish his national defense credentials and a "mission accomplished" war presidency, which advisors believed would reelect Bush in 2004? Was it, as some claimed, an effort by those embarrassed by Vietnam War losses to erase its stain and reassert military might, all the while building muscle for lucrative defense spending? Was it, as one British officer thought, a "grudge match" between Bush and Saddam?

No one knows. What we do know is that the reasons given for the war were untrue. And we know that these reasons were known—or should have been known—to be untrue by the president.

The mistake cannot be undone. More than 2,500 Americans have died in Iraq, and they cannot be brought back to life. More than 15,000 Americans have been injured in Iraq, and their bodies cannot be made whole. Hundreds of billions of dollars spent on the war were siphoned away from desperately needed programs here at home—student loans, affordable housing, health care—and created another class of victims. The losses to the Iraqi people have been staggering—and they cannot be reclaimed.

Because the burdens of war are so enormous, the right of a free people to make that decision cannot be taken away. Creating a fallacious threat sabotages the right of Congress and the right of the people to understand and assess the real facts and to sort through the options carefully and intelligently.

As a result of the false assertions by the president and his administration, many Americans believed that we had to attack Iraq to protect our shores from another attack. People also thought that we were justified in doing so because Saddam was responsible for the 9/11 attacks, based on what they heard from their president and his team. The people overwhelmingly supported the invasion of Iraq, and the House of Representatives and the Senate voted for invasion by strong majorities. Now that these false rationales have been unmasked, support for the war has plummeted. Most Americans, in poll after poll, believe the war was a mistake.

Plainly, the president's false claims tipped the balance toward support of the war. While most Americans and members of Congress would have approved the toppling of Saddam Hussein or the start of democracy in Iraq, that is not the same as agreeing to fight a war to accomplish these ends.

Defrauding Congress and the American people into supporting a war is an impeachable offense. These actions violate the constitutional system of checks and balances and subvert our democracy.

BACKGROUND ON CONSTITUTIONAL LIMITATIONS AND WAR POWERS

The framers of the Constitution understood the costs of war. They also knew that monarchs, or executives, were much more likely than a legislative body to embroil a country in war.

At the end of the 1970s, years after the end of the Vietnam War, I traveled to Southeast Asia several times as the chair of the House Subcommittee on Immigration, Refugees and International Law to work on refugee concerns. From Hanoi to Phnom Pen, I saw the sad remnants of the war. Bomb craters pockmarked the Hanoi airport and the Vietnamese people, impoverished, went shoeless. Cambodia, still recovering from the ruthless Pol Pot regime, had more cattle than people walking its city streets. Refugee camps were filled with children who had lost their parents and their homes. The devastation and dislocation of war spread to every corner and was impossible to ignore.

The founders of our nation wanted to make it harder for the country to go to war. After fighting the British in the war of independence, they were leery of war powers. So, while they designated the president as the commander in chief of the army and the navy in order to assure effective implementation of decisions to go to war, they gave Congress—and not the president—the power to declare war, raise armies, provide for the common defense and fund a war. (See Appendices B, C.) Because the legislative branch was closer to the people, they reasoned that representatives would have to explain to their constituents why the costs of war should be incurred and their taxes used in that way. The legislature would be more reluctant to act except in cases of clear necessity.

James Madison explained the thinking in a 1798 letter to Thomas Jefferson: "The Constitution supposes what the history of all government demonstrates, that the executive is the branch of power most interested in war and most prone to it. It has accordingly with studied care vested the question of war in the legislative."

Similarly, Alexander Hamilton, a key advocate of a strong president, stated, "War is a question, under our constitution, not of executive, but of legislative cognizance. It belongs to Congress to say whether the nation shall of choice dismiss the olive branch or unfurl the banners of war." In Federalist Paper Number 69, he emphasized that the distinction between the British king and the U.S. president lies in the king's power to declare war and raise armies, something not granted to the president.

Even President George Washington was forced to go to Congress when he wanted to prosecute the war against the Indians, despite his status as a hero general who won the Revolutionary War. Washington had to return to Congress repeatedly to get more troops.

But when a president deceives the Congress and the American people, he deprives them of the ability to determine whether the proposed war is worth the costs in life and treasure.

As mentioned earlier, during the Watergate hearings, I prepared an impeachment article based on President Nixon's secret bombing of Cambodia and Representative John Conyers introduced it. It called for the impeachment of the president for ordering the bombing and concealing it from Congress. (See Appendix F.)

The secret bombings had begun in 1969. Under President Nixon's direction, fake records were created on bombing targets, and top officials made false and misleading statements to the Congress about the bombing campaign. The policy of deception continued for more than four years.

Twenty-one members of the House Judiciary Committee—a majority—believed that the president had usurped Congress's power to declare war. In the end, twelve representatives, including me, voted in support of the article of impeachment based on this illegal activity. Nine members issued a commentary showing that they believed a president's overreaching on war powers was a proper subject for impeachment, but were voting against the article because they felt Congress had remedied the situation by passing the War Powers Resolution in 1973, requiring the president to notify Congress of war making activity. They also suggested that Congress may well have gone along with the bombing, as it had with so much of the Vietnam War, but added, "Impeachment of a President should not be foreclosed in situations where Congress was forced by events to support a military venture initiated by a President acting in excess of his authority; indeed, such actions go to the very heart of the Constitutional allocation of powers."

I, along with several other Committee members, believed this article of impeachment to be one of the most serious. We issued a joint statement about our reasons for supporting it: "The decision to make war has enormous human, economic and ethical implications. It is intolerable in a constitutional democracy to permit that decision to be made in secret by a President and to be hidden through deception from the law-making bodies and the public."

President Nixon argued that other presidents had lied to Congress about war activities, so he was no different. This, of course, is no justification for wrongdoing, and from my perspective, only heightened the need to hold Nixon accountable and prevent future presidents from making the same claim.

"This Committee has firmly rejected the notion that because other Presidents may have abused their powers, the abuses of President Nixon are acceptable," several of us wrote in a statement supporting the article. "We should make it clear that Presidential lying and deception, in derogation of the Constitutional powers of Congress, are intolerable."

As I look back, it seems that many Committee members who did not support this article of impeachment had a pragmatic reason in mind. They feared that the resolution might appear to be a political disagreement over the war—and not over war making powers. Since so many other decisive grounds existed for impeachment, they didn't want to risk losing support for them by appearing to politicize the process.

Given what we now know about the war in Iraq, the conclusion to our statement in support of Nixon's impeachment for the secret Cambodia bombing still resonates.

The sole remedy which Congress can employ to bring a President to account for usurpation of the war-making and appropriations powers is impeachment. Only the use of that power is an effective deterrent; and, failing to employ it, when necessary, sets a dangerous precedent. . . . Secrecy and deception which deny to the Congress its lawful role are destructive of the basic right of the American people to participate in their government's life-and-death decisions. Adoption of Article IV [on Cambodia bombing issues] would give notice to all future Presidents that the American people and the Congress may not be excluded from those decisions.

Some thirty years later, we are faced with another president who has engaged in even more elaborate deceptions and with severe, and fatal, consequences. Now we must reassert, once and for all, the intention of our founders: presidents may not drive us into war based on false pretenses, false information, lies to Congress, and lies to the people.

IMPEACHABLE OFFENSES
IN TAKING THE COUNTRY TO WAR

President Bush told us that there were weapons of mass destruction in Iraq and that Saddam Hussein presented a nuclear threat to us and was in cahoots with al Qaeda and those responsible for 9/11. We know now that these statements were deeply misleading and steeped in falsehoods.

President Bush, personally, made many of these pronouncements. He made them to the U.S. Congress and to the American people. He made them in his State of the Union address in 2003 and to the United Nations in 2002.

These fabrications were used by President Bush to justify the imminent need to go to war in Iraq. A review of available facts and information shows that the president had substantial information at his fingertips and personally presented to him that contradicted the statements he made prior to the start of the war in March 2003. Yet, even though he knew them to be untrue, he deliberately continued to make the false statements. This conduct fails to fulfill his oath of office and constitutes a failure "to take care" that the laws are "faithfully executed."

Presenting misleading and untrue information to Congress and the people about a war is an abuse of power. The people place their trust in the president, and, in delivering false statements leading to war, the president committed impeachable offenses.

EVIDENCE OF PRESIDENTIAL ACTS IN FALSELY PRESSING THE WAR IN IRAQ

Predetermination to Go to War without Cause

In the summer of 2002, nine months before President Bush began the invasion of Iraq and two months before the president's first public declarations indicating an intention to go to war, Sir Richard Dearlove, the British chief of intelligence, visited his counterparts in Washington, D.C. Upon return to London on July 23, 2002, he briefed Prime Minister Tony Blair and other British officials at 10 Downing Street, the official quarters of the prime minister. The Downing Street Minutes, reporting on that discussion, were leaked to the public in May 2005.

Sir Richard said, "Military action is now seen as inevitable. Bush wanted to remove Saddam through military action, justified by the conjunction of terrorism and WMD. *But the intelligence and facts were being fixed around the policy.*" (Emphasis added.)

The Downing Street Minutes underscore that the president and his team intended to fabricate "intelligence and facts" to justify a decision to go to war. As described in the memo, two topics—terrorism and weapons of mass destruction—were to be the centerpiece of a "marketing campaign" to drum up support for an attack on Iraq.

The CIA's highest-ranking officer in Europe at the time, Tyler Drumheller, had the same experience as the British during the run-up to war. He told *60 Minutes* in April 2006, one year after he retired, that in the prewar period, the White House refused to listen to verifiable and credible information from a high-ranking source in Iraq who said that there were no weapons of mass destruction. Said Drumheller, "The policy was set. The war in Iraq was coming. And they were looking for intelligence to fit into the policy, to justify the policy."

Exactly when President Bush decided to invade Iraq is not known, but insider reports cite evidence that planning extended back to the very first weeks after he took office.

Former Treasury Secretary Paul O'Neill recalled that Iraq and regime change were being discussed at the very first National Security Council meeting after Bush became president in January 2001, eight months before the 9/11 attacks. O'Neill remembers that no one discussed the "why" of regime change, just the "how," according to a book about O'Neill by Ron Suskind.

Many key players who joined the administration when Bush took office were already on record as calling for the overthrow of Saddam Hussein through their association with a conservative policy group in Washington, D.C., the Project for the New American Century. On January 26, 1998, members of the group wrote to President Bill Clinton, urging him to "undertake military action" in Iraq with the goal of "removing

Saddam Hussein and his regime from power." If Saddam developed destructive weapons, the letter said, "a significant portion of the world's supply of oil will be put at risk." Signers of the letter included Donald Rumsfeld, who became Bush's secretary of defense; Paul Wolfowitz, who became Rumsfeld's deputy; Richard Perle, who became chair of the Defense Policy Board; James Woolsey, member of the Defense Policy Board, and others. A seventy-six page report released by the Project for the New American Century in 2000 laid out their reasons for regime change in Iraq. The publication described a need to build long-lasting military bases that would allow the United States to project military power in the Middle East. Global leadership in the "energy production region" formed an "essential" mission for America, the report said.

Following the attacks of 9/11, the focus on Iraq intensified.

All of the intelligence reports pointed to the al Qaeda terror network and its leader, Osama bin Laden. Only weeks before the attack, as reported by the bipartisan 9/11 Commission, the president had been warned in his daily intelligence briefing about al Qaeda with the headline: "bin Laden determined to strike in the U.S." There was no connection between bin Laden, a Saudi who operated from Afghanistan, and Iraq.

Despite the role of al Qaeda in the 9/11 attack, members of the Bush administration turned immediately to striking Iraq. At a meeting on September 12, Secretary of Defense Rumsfeld twice suggested bombing Iraq, saying there were good targets there, not in Afghanistan. Paul Wolfowitz also argued for holding Iraq responsible for the attacks, according to Richard Clarke, then the White House expert on terrorism.

Clarke recounted in a *60 Minutes* interview on March 21, 2004, that President Bush called him over on the day after the 9/11 attacks and personally said to him, "I want you to find whether Iraq did this." Clarke reported his response: "I said, 'Mr. President. . . . There's no connection.' He came back at me and said, 'Iraq! Saddam! Find out if there's a connection.'" Clarke gathered the top intelligence experts in the FBI and CIA, and sent a memo the next day to the president, repeating that the government experts found no connection between the 9/11 attack and Saddam. The memo was returned to Clarke by the office of the national security advisor with the comment: "Wrong answer. . . . Do it again."

Even as the United States first struck against al Qaeda in Afghanistan on October 7, 2001, insiders understood that there would be a second phase—a war in Iraq—although this information was hidden from the public. Inside the administration, attention turned too quickly to Iraq. Although the weak Taliban government in Afghanistan crumbled readily, the U.S. military did not fully attain its objectives. Osama bin Laden escaped, and the al Qaeda network remains a threat to the United States.

Despite the unfinished business in Afghanistan, by early 2002, President Bush made his decision to "take out" Saddam, according to former Treasury Secretary O'Neill. In March 2002, concealed from Congress and the American people, U.S. troops and military equipment were pulled away from Afghanistan and redeployed to attack Iraq. On March 14, 2002—over dinner—Condoleezza Rice let British envoy David Manning know that the United States was planning a military campaign against Iraq with the goal of "regime change," according to documents leaked in 2005. On March 25, 2002, British Secretary of State Jack Straw warned Prime Minister Blair that an upcoming meeting with President Bush at his ranch in April would focus on taking military action in Iraq, according to another leaked memo. While the decision to invade Iraq had been made in secret much earlier, the public relations campaign to convince the American public and Congress to go along with it was not launched until fall 2002. By the time of the first anniversary of the World Trade Center and Pentagon attacks, the administration had fully "fixed" its attention on a war in Iraq.

THE FIRST DECEPTION: IRAQ IS ALLIED WITH AL QAEDA AND BEHIND 9/11

At the time of the U.S. invasion of Iraq on March 19, 2003, polls indicated that two-thirds of the American people believed that Saddam Hussein had instigated the 9/11 attacks in the United States.

Soldiers, dressed in their sand fatigues and riding their armored vehicles into Iraq , repeated a similar refrain to television reporters: "Payback for 9/11."

President Bush and the highest officials in his administration successfully convinced people of a connection between al Qaeda and 9/11, even though none existed.

On September 25, 2002, President Bush said, "You can't distinguish between al Qaeda and Saddam." He elaborated in his speech in Cincinnati on October 7, 2002. Drawing upon the memory of America's "vulnerability" on September 11, 2001, the president said Iraq posed a threat and that Iraq had weapons of mass destruction (a falsehood). "And that is the source of our urgent concern about Saddam Hussein's links to international terrorist groups," the president continued. "We know that Iraq and the al Qaeda terrorist network share a common enemy—the United States of America. We know that Iraq and al Qaeda have had high-level contacts that go back a decade. Some al Qaeda leaders who fled Afghanistan went to Iraq. . . . Iraq has trained al Qaeda members. . . . And we know that after September the 11th, Saddam Hussein's regime gleefully celebrated the terrorist attacks on America."

Bush invoked September 11th five times in his speech on the war on Iraq. The al Qaeda network is mentioned by name at least five times (although never Osama bin Laden, still at large), and the words "terror" and "terrorists" appear so often as to resemble punctuation marks. "Iraq could decide on any given day to provide a biological or chemical weapon to a terrorist group or individual terrorists. Alliance with terrorists could allow the Iraqi regime to attack America," he said. "Failure to act would . . . allow terrorists access to new weapons and new resources."

By implying that Saddam was somehow responsible for the 9/11 attacks, the administration sought to build public support and justify the war as retaliation.

Cementing Sadaam and al Qaeda together also allowed President Bush to suggest that Saddam would provoke attacks directly on the United States by providing terrorists with weapons of mass destruction. Otherwise, the question would inevitably arise as to how a nuclear bomb would make its way from Iraq to U.S. shores, since all agreed that Saddam had no long-range ballistic missiles. The administration tried to overcome this obstacle by arguing that Saddam would hand his nuclear weapons over to terrorists, specifically al Qaeda.

The insistence that a link existed began surfacing in September 2002, along with the promotion of other war rationales. On September 19, 2002, Secretary Rumsfeld told the Senate Armed Services Committee: "We know al Qaeda is operating in Iraq today and that little happens without the knowledge of Saddam Hussein regime." A little more than week later, on September 27 in a speech at a Chamber of Commerce lunch in Atlanta, Rumsfeld said had "bulletproof" evidence of Saddam–al Qaeda links. (One month later, in a press briefing, he explained that he was relying on the CIA and "five or six sentences that were bulletproof.") National Security Advisor Rice listed supposed al Qaeda and Iraq contacts on *The News Hour* on September 25, 2002, and concluded, "There's a relationship here."

Vice President Cheney played a substantial role in making the false Saddam–Al Qaeda connection. On August 26, 2002, Cheney said in a speech: "Many of us are convinced that Saddam Hussein will acquire nuclear weapons fairly soon," and these, said Cheney, could go to terrorists. It was, the vice president, told us, "as grave a threat as can be imagined." Both before and after the invasion, Cheney insisted that one of the 9/11 hijackers had met with an Iraqi agent, even though that possibility was discredited by intelligence agencies and the 9/11 commission.

Secretary of State Powell used a substantial portion of his speech to the UN Security Council on February 5, 2003, to argue the Saddam–al Qaeda connection, a series of falsehoods which he called a "sinister nexus between Iraq and the al Qaeda terrorist network." Iraq hosted training camps for al Qaeda, provided special information about chemical and biological weapons, and harbored al Qaeda members, Powell said. "This . . . builds on decades long experience with respect to ties between Iraq and al Qaeda," he said. Powell underscored in his speech that everything he said was accurate. "Every statement I make today is backed up by solid sources. These are not assertions. We are giving you facts and conclusions based on solid evidence. This is evidence, not conjecture. This is true." But what he said was not true.

The president personally continued to link the activities of Saddam and al Qaeda.

In his January 2003 State of the Union address, President Bush said, "Evidence from intelligence sources, secret communications, and statements by people now in custody reveal that Saddam Hussein aids and protects terrorists, including members of al Qaeda." Fostering the frightening image of an alliance, the president said, "Imagine those nineteen hijackers . . . this time armed by Saddam Hussein. . . . It would take one vial, one canister, one crate into this country to bring a day of horror like one we have never known. We will do everything in our power to make sure that day never comes."

Speaking to a reporter on January 31, 2003, the president said information about Iraq shows "al Qaeda links that really do portend a danger for America and for Great Britain, anybody else who loves freedom."

On February 8, 2003, in a radio address, President Bush listed a series of supposed contacts between Iraq and al Qaeda. "Saddam Hussein has longstanding, direct and continuing ties to terrorist networks. . . . Iraq has also provided Al Qaeda with chemical and biological weapons training," he said.

On March 17, 2003, just two days before the United States began its invasion of Iraq, the president gave a televised address to the nation from the White House. "The danger is clear: Using chemical, biological, or, one day, nuclear weapons obtained with the help of Iraq, the terrorists could fulfill their stated ambitions and kill thousands or hundreds of thousands of innocent people in our country."

Aside from rhetoric to draw support for the planned invasion, President Bush directly used the concocted alliance between Saddam and al Qaeda as the underlying basis for authorization to take military action.

On March 18, 2003, President Bush sent a letter to Congress, containing a formal notice of the start of the war against Iraq. In this "letter of determination," the president declared that the war met the conditions of the October 2002 congressional resolution supporting the use of military force. Congress had specifically permitted the president to take future military action in Iraq if a link were shown connecting the action to 9/11.

In his official capacity, the president told Congress that the use of armed forces against Iraq "is consistent with the United States and other countries continuing to take the necessary actions against international terrorists and terrorist organizations, including those nations, organizations or persons who planned, authorized, committed, or aided the terrorist attacks that occurred on September 11, 2001."

After the war in Iraq had already begun, the bipartisan 9/11 Commission explicitly found that there was no basis for claiming any connection between al Qaeda and Saddam. In its June 2004 release, the Commission found no "collaborative" relationship between Iraq and al Qaeda and "no credible evidence that Iraq and al Qaeda cooperated on attacks against the United States."

The Senate Select Committee Report on Pre-War Intelligence found "no evidence" of Iraqi complicity with or assistance to al Qaeda. David Kay, U.S. weapons inspector, said there was no sharing of weapons of mass destruction.

Accumulating documentation shows that the Saddam–al Qaeda axis was disproven long before the war started and that the president had direct knowledge that no link existed.

In addition to firsthand information from antiterrorism expert Richard Clarke immediately following 9/11, the president's briefing on September 21, 2001, reported that there was no complicity between Saddam and al Qaeda. "President Bush was told in a highly classified brief that the U.S. intelligence community had no evidence linking the Iraqi regime of Saddam Hussein to the attacks," according to investigative reporter Murray Waas of *The National Journal*, who said he reviewed government records and spoke with officials directly involved.

In June 2002, the CIA reported that there was "no conclusive evidence of cooperation," according to a Report of the Select Committee on U.S. Intelligence. The October 2002 National Intelligence Estimate (NIE) declared that the combined intelligence agencies had "low confidence" in any likelihood that Saddam would share weapons of mass destruction with al Qaeda. This point was emphasized by naming it a "Key Judgment." The remote likelihood of sharing would arise only if Saddam were under attack and, even then, it was far-fetched. Saddam would have to be "sufficiently desperate," the NIE said. Of primary importance is that this critical piece of information was omitted from the version of the NIE document delivered to Congress and released to the public, according to a comparison by the Carnegie Endowment for International Peace after portions of the classified NIE were released in July 2003.

On January 29, 2003, nearly two months before the invasion of Iraq, the CIA released a report stating that no Iraqi training of al Qaeda actually occurred and that all of the claims about training were based on hearsay and lacked substantiation. It affirmed and strengthened a similar statement in the October 2002 NIE.

In October 2004, Secretary Rumsfeld, in questioning at the Council of Foreign Relations in New York, revised his prewar commentary about the supposed Saddam–al Qaeda alliance. "To my knowledge, I have not seen any strong, hard evidence that links the two," he said. It was a rare admission.

The president and his team have inconsistently tried to reassert the disproven claims that Saddam and ad Qaeda are connected and continue, on the other hand, to cover up and deny the verbal trail that follows them.

In his May 2003 "Mission Accomplished" speech aboard an aircraft carrier, the president said major combat in Iraq had ended (despite continuing war activities) and declared, "We have removed an ally of al Qaeda."

When the president was questioned at an Ohio forum in March 2006 about his claims that Saddam was linked to the 9/11 attacks, he had a different spin. "First—just if I might correct a misperception, I don't think we ever said, at least I know I didn't say that there was a direct connection between September 11 and Saddam Hussein," the president said. Yet, the president justified the war to Congress, as a "necessary" action against those who "planned, authorized, committed, or aided the terrorist attacks that occurred on September 11, 2001."

This use of false information to begin and carry out a war is a serious violation of the president's Oath of Office.

THE SECOND DECEPTION: SADDAM
AND NUCLEAR WEAPONS

The possibility of a nuclear strike on America sounded especially ominous to a still jittery nation after 9/11. In September 2002, the Bush administration methodically drilled in the idea that Saddam Hussein was intent on a nuclear attack on the United States and had the means to carry it out.

The president and his team falsely claimed that Saddam had nuclear weapon capacity. Their "proof" was twofold: first, Saddam was acquiring aluminum tubes to be used for enriching uranium; second, Saddam was buying yellowcake uranium for weapons. Both items are essential physical elements in the complicated and years-long process of building a nuclear weapon. Both claims, as we now know, were false.

Fears about Iraq's nuclear capacity were set in motion on September 7, 2002, when British Prime Minister Blair and President George W. Bush appeared jointly before the press at Camp David. Blair referred to a new report from the International Atomic Energy Agency, showing that Saddam Hussein was getting nuclear weapons. "The threat from Saddam Hussein and weapons of mass destruction—chemical, biological, potentially nuclear-weapons capability—the threat is real," Blair said.

President Bush echoed him. The IAEA report indicates, the president said, Iraqis are "six months away from developing a [nuclear] weapon." The president added, "I don't know what more evidence we need."

One problem. There was no such IAEA report. It was a total fiction. The White House later acknowledged that it did not exist. Moreover, the last IAEA report in 1999 reiterated evidence that Iraq had dismantled its nuclear weapons program. The U.S. National Intelligence Estimate (NIE) from December 2001 agreed.

The nuclear imagery was ushered in again on October 7, 2002, when President Bush delivered a speech about Iraq in Cincinnati: "America must not ignore the threat gathering against us. Facing clear evidence of peril, we cannot wait for the final proof—the smoking gun—that could come in the form of a mushroom cloud," he said.

The information that the majority of U.S. intelligence agencies did not believe that Saddam had nuclear weapons was concealed from the public.

In private, President Bush admitted that there were no weapons of mass destruction (WMD) in Iraq. Six weeks before the start of the war, on January 31, 2003, President Bush and Prime Minister Blair met. A memorandum was made of the meeting and leaked much later to British legal scholar Phillipe Sands, author of *Lawless World*. The *New York Times* also reviewed and verified the memorandum. According to the memo, President Bush acknowledged to Blair that Iraq had no WMD. Bush said the war would start in March, in any case, and the two discussed alternate ways of rationalizing the war—one of Bush's ideas was to paint a plane in UN colors and provoke Saddam into firing at it. Yet, only three days earlier, the president had told the Congress and the American people in his State of the Union message that Iraq was a nuclear threat.

Instead of providing a truthful picture or full information of Iraq's weapons of mass destruction, the president and his team pursued a path of deliberate, elaborate, and concerted deception designed to drive the country to war.

False Statements about Aluminum Tubes and Iraq

Promotion of the idea that Saddam Hussein was acquiring aluminum tubes for a nuclear weapons program received a solid blastoff in September 2002.

On CNN, Condolezza Rice insisted that Iraq had aluminum tubes which were "only really suited for nuclear weapons programs." This statement was false.

At approximately the same time, on September 8, 2002, Vice President Cheney said on *Meet the Press,* "I know with absolutely certainty that he [Saddam] is using his procurement system to acquire the equipment he needs to enrich uranium to build a nuclear weapon." This was false.

The president himself spoke on this topic to the United Nations General Assembly on September 12, 2002. He, too, emphasized the purchase of aluminum tubes. "Iraq has made several attempts to buy high-strength aluminum tubes used to enrich uranium for a nuclear weapon," the president said. This statement was false, as well.

Aluminum tubes en route to Iraq had been intercepted by intelligence agencies. But the key experts and authorities in the Bush administration did not believe that they could be used to enrich uranium.

The Department of Energy, the State Department, the International Atomic Energy Agency, British intelligence, and even the Defense Department intelligence division all agreed that the tubes were intended for conventional rockets, and not for nuclear weapons. The Department of Energy, the lead agency on nuclear weapons, had scientific experts who actually examined the intercepted tubes. The tubes' dimensions were wrong for use as uranium centrifuges and they were anodized, which would create an adverse chemical reaction with uranium. On the other hand, the tubes were consistent with use in rockets—the dimensions were virtually identical to those of an Italian rocket and very similar to rockets used by the United States.

A ninety-six page classified National Intelligence Estimate (NIE), a critically important document, was delivered to the president and other key Bush administration officials in October 2002. Titled "Key Judgments from the National Intelligence Estimate on Iraq's Continuing Programs for Weapons of Mass Destruction," it described the analysis of the aluminum tubes by the six intelligence agencies involved in national security issues on Iraq. The State Department's experts wrote that they were "not persuaded that the tubes in question are intended for use as centrifuge rotors" and the agency "accepts the judgment of technical experts at the U.S. Department of Energy (DOE) who have concluded that the tubes Iraq seeks to acquire are poorly suited for use in gas centrifuges to be used for uranium enrichment and finds unpersuasive the arguments advanced by others. . . . The tubes are not intended for use in Iraq's nuclear weapon program."

One agency—the CIA—disagreed based on the view of a single engineer who had never worked with centrifuges to enrich uranium. The CIA itself had waffled on the claim in four prior reports in 2001 and 2002.

As national security advisor, Rice was certainly aware that the credible experts declared the tubes unsuitable for nuclear material since it was her job to coordinate differences among intelligence agencies.

A one-page President's Summary of the NIE contained the same information and, according to investigative findings by journalist Murray Waas in *The National Journal*, was delivered personally to the president by CIA Director George Tenet. To date, President Bush has refused to release the president's summary or the full text of the ninety-six- page report.

The public did not know that the key experts inside the government disagreed with the statements that the president was making.

In a major speech on Iraq from Cincinnati on October 7, 2002, less than one week after receiving the NIE, President Bush declared, "Iraq has attempted to purchase high-strength aluminum tubes and other equipment needed for gas centrifuges." He did not explain that this was not the view of the majority of U.S. intelligence agencies.

Although the International Atomic Energy Agency said on January 27, 2003, that the aluminum tubes would not be suitable for nuclear uses, the president, in his State of the

Union Message on January 28, 2003, used the tubes to claim that Saddam was building nuclear weapons. "Our intelligence sources tell us that [Saddam] has attempted to purchase high-strength aluminum tubes suitable for nuclear weapons production," the president said in solemn tones. The president had more than enough evidence to know it was not true.

The next week, in February 2003, Secretary of State Colin Powell referred to the aluminum tubes in a speech to the UN. Powell said the tubes were suited for nuclear uses, disregarding the explicit advice of his own agency. His statement was false.

The administration's public statements also were accompanied by a disinformation campaign to mislead Congress.

A declassified version of the October 2002 NIE was prepared with an alteration in the conclusions of the national security agencies. It falsely stated that: "*All intelligence experts agree* that Iraq is seeking nuclear weapons and that these tubes could be used in a centrifuge enrichment program" (emphasis added). But, despite that conclusion, the Department of Energy and State Department did not join in this assessment.

The disinformation campaign also led to selective leaking to the press. At the same time that the administration was rolling out its war marketing, the *New York Times* published an article that relied heavily on anonymous Bush administration sources who said that Iraq was purchasing aluminum tubes "meant for a nuclear weapons program." Headlined "U.S. Says Hussein Intensified Quest for A-Bomb Parts," the

September 8, 2002, story by Judith Miller and Michael Gordon asserted that Saddam had "embarked on a worldwide hunt for materials to make an atomic bomb," and repeated the administration's false claims. Much later—more than a year after the invasion—the newspaper apologized for its lack of skepticism toward the administration sources who had hyped a nonexistent threat.

President Bush had direct information that Iraq was not developing centrifuges. But rather than present a clear and accurate assessment of the threat to Congress or the American people, he misstated the danger and created a false picture of the need for a war.

False Statements about Uranium and Iraq

Even if aluminum tubes were available, nuclear weapons rely upon fissile material, specifically uranium. President Bush declared repeatedly that Iraq had acquired uranium, or was trying to do so. This was untrue, as he knew or had reason to know.

The president declared in his January 28, 2003 State of the Union message: "The British government has learned that Saddam Hussein recently sought significant quantities of uranium from Africa."

But the Bush administration knew for more than a year that this claim about Saddam was utterly untrue.

The story that Iraq was purchasing five hundred tons of uranium in Niger originated in Italy with documents that were repeatedly shown to be fakes and thoroughly worthless.

The story was not "recent," as the president said, since the documents were dated in 2000. The CIA and State Department both found the uranium claim baseless. So did the International Atomic Energy Agency.

The National Intelligence Estimate of October 2002 in its long form carried a statement from the State Department's Bureau of Intelligence and Research (INR) that "the claims of Iraqi pursuit of natural uranium in Africa are, in INR's assessment, highly dubious." According to a top White House official, the president was frequently briefed on the contents of the NIE. "The President has been briefed on . . . countless occasions about the contents of the NIE," said the official in a July 18, 2003, session with reporters about the uranium claim. Anonymous insider accounts given to journalist Murray Waas at the *National Journal* state that Tenet personally briefed President Bush on the uranium claim.

At the request of the CIA, the French government checked out the story and found it to be false. In addition, a U.S. general and our then ambassador to Niger found it to be untrue. In February 2002, the CIA asked former Ambassador Joseph Wilson IV to go to Niger to investigate. He did so, and he also reported that the Niger uranium story was false.

The CIA tried to put the brakes on the use of the uranium claim. In October 2002, George Tenet was so concerned about the falsity of the Niger uranium claim that he called the White House personally to make sure it was taken out of a speech the president planned to give in Cincinnati on October 7, 2002. Tenet followed up with letters, one to

National Security Advisor Condoleezza Rice and two to Stephen J. Hadley, deputy national security advisor. The claim was removed from the speech. Nonetheless, the president said in his Cincinnati address: "Evidence indicates that Iraq is reconstituting its nuclear weapons program." This, of course, could not happen without access to uranium, and although the direct reference to uranium was removed, the false impression remained.

In December 2002, the International Atomic Energy Agency wrote to the White House, challenging the validity of the uranium claim. The State Department sent a memo to the White House in January 2003 to emphasize that the Niger uranium claim was untrue. At one point, the State Department ridiculed the claim, noting that a transfer of five hundred tons of uranium product would necessitate twenty-five tractor trailers going across the desert, something not likely to be missed, but also "difficult in the extreme" because of wear and tear on vehicles, 150-degree heat, drifting sand, and lack of water and fuel. Also in January, the National Intelligence Council, at the request of the Pentagon, delivered a definitive judgment to the White House, stating point-blank that the Niger story was not true, according to Barton Gellman and Dafna Linzer in the *Washington Post* on April 9, 2006.

Yet the uranium claim reappeared in the president's State of the Union message on January 28, 2003, to bolster the argument that Saddam was building nuclear weapons.

If the president had not read the statements by the IAEA, the Defense Department, the State Department, or National

Intelligence Council or listened to his NIE briefings or his daily intelligence briefings, he was immediately put on notice that something was wrong when the British were cited in his speech, but no U.S. intelligence agency was mentioned. At that point, the president had, in his hand, evidence that something was fishy. As a reporter said to a White House official in a transcribed July 2003 press briefing, "you must have known that there was some problem, otherwise we'd use good old USA intelligence." The events show that the president either knew that the claim was false or closed his eyes to finding the truth.

Months after the invasion of Iraq when criticism arose, the president acknowledged that the uranium statement ("sixteen words") should not have been in his State of Union address. At first CIA Director Tenet took the blame for his agency's failure to remove the "sixteen words." When information came to light about the CIA's much earlier warnings that this claim was wrong, Rice's deputy, Stephen Hadley, said it was his fault for leaving the "sixteen words" in, despite the direct warnings to him by the CIA in October. "I should have recalled . . . that there was controversy associated with the uranium issues," he said. "It is now clear to me that I failed." After their respective mea culpas, Tenet was awarded the presidential Medal of Freedom and Rice and Hadley were promoted to secretary of state and national security advisor, respectively.

The president's failure to demand accountability from Rice and Hadley demonstrates that he knew full well about the falsity of the uranium claim. Promoting them suggests not that they performed badly at their jobs by providing the president with false information about a critical point, but that they did what they were supposed to do—make "a case" for war, even if that meant using false information.

Before the invasion of Iraq, on March 7, 2003, the IAEA reported to the UN that the uranium story was based on forgeries and was not to be believed.

The president's false statement about uranium has also entwined the White House in a criminal indictment. After former Ambassador Joseph Wilson accused the president of "twisting" the information in July 2003, one or more administration officials divulged the identity of Wilson's wife, a covert CIA agent, a potential crime. (See Chapter Seven.) A top aide, I. Lewis Libby, assistant to the president for national security, has been indicted.

OTHER DECEPTIONS

The president and his team used other serious deceptions and false statements to take the American public down its war path. A complete list of misinformation used in run-up to the Iraq War would fill a much larger volume.

Four other areas of deception bear mentioning: the hyping of biological weaponry in Iraq; the refusal to heed UN weapons inspectors, who turned out to be remarkably accurate; the painting of a false picture of the reception Americans would receive in Iraq; and the deliberate efforts to mislead people about the costs and length of the war.

Massive Biological and Chemical Weaponry

The Bush administration misrepresented Iraq's arsenal of biological and chemical weapons, often presenting minimal risks as grave threats and using fictional scenarios to portray an immediate danger to the American people.

"Senior administration officials show a very systematic misrepresentation of the facts over and above the intelligence failings, with respect to chemical and biological weapons," reported a researcher with the Carnegie Endowment for International Peace, which analyzed the administration's claims on biological and chemical weaponry in Iraq.

Prior to the war, Secretary Rumsfeld told the House Armed Services Committee that biological weapons posed an immediate danger to the United States because they would be passed to terrorists who would use them to attack the United States. On September 18, 2002, Rumsfeld said Saddam could release "sleeper cells armed with biological weapons to attack us from within."

Secretary of State Powell described in his February 2003 speech to the UN Iraq's fancy aerial balloons—blimps—that were going to be used to spread biological and chemical weapons beyond Iraq's borders. There were none. As a centerpiece of his presentation, he displayed large, blown-up photos of supposed mobile biological weapons laboratories; slides showed detailed mockups. Powell said that "in a single month" the mobile labs could make weapons-grade microbes "to kill thousands upon thousands of people." There were no mobile weapons laboratories. The information was based solely on a defector in Germany, and the West Germans had advised the United States that his information was unreliable. A raft of reports by U.S. and other intelligence agencies called the defector, dubbed Curveball, a "fabricator" and "problematic" and "out of control." In December 2001, when the Pentagon sent a CIA agent to give him a lie detector test, he flunked.

The president also made a number of misleading comments about biological weapons. "Right now, Iraq is expanding and improving facilities that were used for the production of biological weapons," he said to the UN General Assembly on September 12, 2002.

In Cincinnati on October 7, 2002, the president stretched the extent of Iraq's biological weapons capacity beyond recognition. According to the Carnegie Endowment, inspectors had reported that Iraq had a small amount of biological growth medium that was not a danger in of itself. It had not been used. If used, it could produce a large amount of anthrax. The president altered this finding to state that Iraq had already "likely produced" a massive stockpile of anthrax, which was not true. He said, "This is a massive stockpile of biological weapons that has never been accounted for and is capable of killing millions." The Carnegie Endowment noted, "Small changes like these can easily transform a threat from minor to dire."

U.S. intelligence agencies had a mixed perspective on whether Saddam possessed an arsenal of active biological or chemical weapons. In September 2002, the Defense

Intelligence Agency issued a report that said Iraq's chemical warfare capability was destroyed between 1991 and 1998. There was, it said, "no reliable information" of present capacity. In 1995, a high-level defector, Saddam's son-in-law, Hussein Kamel, reported that Iraq had destroyed all chemical weapons.

Whatever limited information pointed to possible biological or chemical weapons, the Bush administration exaggerated and misstated the threats, trying to instill a sense of imminent danger directly aimed at Americans.

UN inspectors discredited any danger prior to the invasion of Iraq. After conducting 731 inspections in Iraq from November 27, 2002, to March 18, 2003, no biological or chemicals weapon menace was uncovered. They did not find mobile laboratories or aerial balloons or biological weapons or chemical weapons. The inspectors reported no "evidence of the continuation or resumption of programs of weapons of mass destruction or significant quantities of proscribed items."

Since the invasion in March 2003, no biological or chemical weapons have been uncovered in Iraq, despite an extensive search.

Ignored the Work of Inspectors

In January 2003, the International Atomic Energy Agency (IAEA) released a report, declaring that Iraq was not a nuclear threat.

In fall 2002, Saddam Hussein had permitted UN weapons inspectors to reenter Iraq. This action surprised the president and others in his administration who had insisted that Saddam's failure to allow inspectors back into the country proved the necessity of military invasion. The president refused to accept the findings of the UN inspectors and refused to allow them to finish their work.

President Bush insisted, "Sadaam Hussein is fooling the world, or trying to fool the world."

On January 31, 2003, while inspectors were still in Iraq, President Bush made it clear in a White House meeting with British Prime Minister Blair that the war was on, even if the IAEA and UN inspectors failed to find weapons of mass destruction, according to a memo leaked to British author and international law professor Philippe Sands.

Director-General Mohamed ElBaradei of the IAEA reported again to the UN in March 7, 2003, prior to the U.S. invasion of Iraq that inspectors found no evidence that Iraq was "reconstituting its nuclear program." Vice President Cheney belittled the inspectors, and said that they had been wrong before, implying that the United States had secret and better information (although, if so, he did not explain why it wasn't provided to the inspectors).

Inspectors were forced to abandon their work in March 2003, when President Bush began a military invasion.

Despite this, the president has since asserted, untruthfully, that Saddam refused to allow weapons inspectors to return to Iraq. In response to a question by longtime reporter Helen Thomas in March 2006 about why he invaded Iraq, the president said, "The world said [to Saddam], 'Disarm, disclose, or face serious consequences.' . . . And when he chose to deny inspectors, when he chose not to disclose, then I had the difficult decision to make to remove him."

Letting the inspectors complete their work could have been an important aid to peaceful resolution without the loss of lives. As former weapons inspector Scott Ritter told CNN in September 2002: "We're talking about war here. . . . Let's get inspectors back in, let's get them to find out what the ultimate disposition of these weapons programs are, and if Iraq has no weapons of mass destruction program, thank goodness, we just defused a war."

Extensive U.S. inspections after the invasion confirmed the accuracy of the IAEA and UN inspectors, and no weapons of mass destruction have been found.

Americans Would Be Treated as Liberators

Vice President Cheney said Americans will be "greeted as liberators" in Iraq before the start of the war in March 2003. Americans heard repeatedly that the Iraqi population would enthusiastically support an invasion and there would be no popular resistance.

In his State of the Union speech on January 28, 2003, President Bush had a message for the people of Iraq: "The day that [Saddam] and his regime are removed from power will be the day of your liberation."

Many Iraqis did not agree.

A guerrilla movement quickly developed, fueled by remnants of Saddam's army and Sunni concerns about losing their privileged status. Flowers were not strewn, but improvised explosive devices were. Since the president declared the end of major combat operations on May 1, 2003, more than two thousand five hundred American soldiers and two hundred soldiers from other countries, fighting alongside the Americans, have been killed.

All of this was foreseen. (See Chapter Six.) In a coauthored essay in *Time* magazine on March 2, 1998, President Bush's father and his National Security Advisor Brent Scowcroft explained their reasons for not invading Iraq as part of the Persian Gulf War in 1991: "Had we gone the invasion route, the U.S. could conceivably still be an occupying power in a bitterly hostile land. It would have been a dramatically different—and perhaps barren—outcome."

Before the Iraq war in 2003, the intelligence community of George W. Bush also had predicted the very scenario the United States experienced after the invasion, but the president and his top aides ignored or hid the information. Paul R. Pillar, who served as national intelligence officer for the Near East from 2000–2005 reported in *Foreign Affairs* in March/April 2006 that the intelligence services projected "a long, difficult and turbulent transition." Intelligence analysts forecast a deeply divided society, a significant chance of violent conflict, guerrilla warfare, and that "a foreign occupying force would itself be the target of resentment and attacks." They also cast doubt upon the notions that Iraq would be a fertile ground for democracy or that invasion would have a positive effect on the region.

"More likely, war and occupation would boost political
Islam," Pillar said analysts found. "Iraq would become a
magnet for extremists."

The Bush administration failed to inform Congress or the
public of these alarming projected consequences, and failed
to develop plans to deal with these projections.

War in Iraq Would be Inexpensive and Painless

"The use of force in Iraq today would last five days or five
weeks or five months. But it certainly isn't going to last any
longer than that," Secretary of Defense Rumsfeld said on
radio in November 2002.

Kenneth Adelman, a member of the Bush administration's
Defense Policy Board, had an even simpler description: the
war will be a "cakewalk," he said.

Americans were repeatedly assured that the war would be
short and limited.

The cost of the war was deliberately lowballed, and the
funds were kept out of the normal budget process. When
Lawrence Lindsay, the president's chief economic advisor
told the *Wall Street Journal* that the war would cost from
$100 to $200 billion dollars, he was booted. Budget Director
Daniels said Lindsay's prediction was wildly high, and he later
put the bill at $50 billion. Much of the cost of the war, Amer-
icans were told, would be recouped from Iraqi oil wells.

General Eric Shinseki, the head of the Joint Chiefs of Staff,
made the mistake of telling the truth to the Senate Armed
Services Committee—that the war and occupation would

require substantially more troops than the Defense Department planned to send. His successor was named early and he was pushed aside.

Claims that the war would be easy or inexpensive were not true. (See Chapter Six.)

By spring 2006, the cost of the war in Iraq was $270 billion, according to the National Priorities Project. The Center for Strategic and Budgetary Assessments said in April 2006 that the costs approach $10 billion a month. The cost easily tripled the $82 billion cost of the entire 1991 Persian Gulf War. And of that amount, the United States directly paid only $7 billion, with the strong international alliance picking up the rest. The total costs to Americans of the current war in Iraq could reach $700 billion in direct expenditures, according to one recent analysis. These costs will detract from other needs of Americans for health care, education, and financial security.

In addition, the real costs are in lives—lives lost, lives damaged, lives interrupted. By spring 2006, more than ten times as many U.S. military personnel were killed in Iraq as in Gulf War I. There is no accurate count for Iraqi civilian casualties.

President Bush, in proposing to take the nation to war in Iraq, failed to be truthful about the real costs and suffering that could be expected.

CONCLUSION: WHY IMPEACHMENT IS NECESSARY BASED ON EVIDENCE OF WAR DECEPTIONS

President Bush authorized a deliberate scheme, based on a pattern of deceit, to drive the country to a war in Iraq.

He and his administration induced the American people and the Congress to support an invasion of Iraq based on claims that we know now to be completely false. The president was the key participant in this scheme. As such, he drew upon and abused the respect and trust the American people naturally have for his office.

Whether President Bush deliberately misstated the threat or failed to investigate the truth of what he was saying, or both, he cannot escape constitutional accountability. If the statements by the president were deliberate lies, impeachment is certainly warranted on that ground. If his statements were not deliberate, but arose from the president's failure to look into the truth of his statements, then he has failed "to take care" that the laws are "faithfully executed" and impeachment is warranted on those grounds.

A plan to force regime change in Iraq existed prior to, and independent of, the events of 9/11. But the president argued for the war based on false statements linking Saddam and the al Qaeda network, and blaming Saddam for 9/11. Strong and credible evidence shows that the president knew that his statements drawing connections between Iraq and 9/11 were false. The president was personally informed on the day after 9/11 by the nation's top counterterrorism expert, Richard Clarke, that Iraq and 9/11 were not connected. This information was repeated in reports by the CIA and other intelligence agencies, which found no reliable connections between al Qaeda and Iraq.

The president also urged immediate military action against Iraq based on false claims that Saddam was building nuclear weapons capability and posed a threat to the United States. The evidence shows that the president knew this was untrue. Six weeks prior to the invasion of Iraq in a meeting with Prime Minister Blair, President Bush acknowledged that were no weapons of mass destruction in Iraq.

Yet, only three days before the Blair meeting, the president delivered his State of the Union address and declared otherwise. Painting a false picture of Iraq as a nuclear threat, he stated that Iraq was purchasing uranium. This statement was untrue, as the president knew or had reason to know from multiple sources.

If the president knew that the uranium claim was untrue, his statement in the State of the Union was a deliberate lie to mislead Congress and the people, an impeachable offense. If the president merely mouthed arguments for the war without giving them thought, that is also an impeachable offense.

The president cannot fall back on ignorance, lack of curiosity, indifference to information, or intellectual laziness when it comes to taking the country to war. The president must inform himself, understand the facts, and weigh the pros and cons before making the momentous decision to go to war; these are requirements of the Oath of Office and his responsibility to uphold the Constitution and to "take care" that the laws are "faithfully executed."

The president has strenuously resisted any congressional inquiry into the use of prewar intelligence by the White House and has refused to declassify the full National Intelligence Estimate of October 2002 or the one-page presidential summary that would give a true picture of what he knew. These actions suggest that the president has something to hide.

On the eve of the war, the president sent a "letter of determination" to Congress, stating that military action was necessary in Iraq to fight against those who caused 9/11, a condition for the authorization of the use of force established by Congress. The president's statement was untrue.

Because of false information from the president, the Congress and the American people were misled about an Iraqi threat and the necessity of war. President Bush abused the trust placed in him, and subverted the constitutional role of Congress.

The president's deceptions to Congress and the American people are high crimes and misdemeanors. Based on deliberate falsehoods, he commenced a war that has resulted in the deaths of more than two thousand five hundred Americans and the injury of many thousands more. For this, he must be removed from office, not only to prevent further abuse of the war making power but also to send a clear and unambiguous signal to future presidents: never again.

CHAPTER FOUR

Impeachment for Illegal Wiretapping and Surveillance of Americans

OVERVIEW

Thousands, and possibly millions, of Americans have been victims of a domestic spying program started by President Bush in 2001 without their knowledge and without the approval of a court.

The déjà-vu of a president's engagement in covert illegal surveillance of Americans took me and many others by complete surprise. We thought we had closed the book on that kind of illegal behavior in the 1970s, with Nixon. Post-Watergate, while I served in the House of Representatives, Congress passed new laws that set out court procedures for approving surveillance deemed necessary for national security, but still respecting the Constitution. This system of court-approved warrants worked well and efficiently.

But President Bush decided to circumvent the law. Beginning in October 2001, he secretly ordered wiretaps of Americans in the United States without seeking court approval. The president took this action in direct contravention of the specific terms of a federal law, the 1978 Foreign Intelligence Surveillance Act (FISA). Violation of FISA is a federal crime. Although the president conducted this program secretly for four years, once exposed, he declared that he has the right to wiretap Americans and would continue to do so without court approval for as long as he thinks is necessary, despite the law.

But President Bush cannot willfully ignore a law that affects basic freedoms and the rights of so many; no president can.

When a president knowingly and deliberately refuses to abide by a law that has important consequences for democracy, or indicates that he will not do so in the future, impeachment is a proper remedy.

BACKGROUND ON THE CONSTITUTION, WIRETAPPING, AND THE FISA LAW

Foreign intelligence surveillance collects intelligence and counterintelligence to protect against espionage, sabotage, and terrorism by foreign governments, foreign agents, terrorists, and associated parties.

The need for foreign intelligence surveillance of terrorists and agents of foreign powers in the United States is not the issue here. That is a given. The question is how the government will meet the need.

Congress answered by passing FISA in 1978, which established a legal system for surveillance in the United States to collect foreign intelligence and U.S. counterintelligence. The law regulates how a president may engage in foreign intelligence surveillance by simply and reasonably requiring court approval.

FISA was enacted against the backdrop of Watergate. Congress saw how unchecked executive branch snooping on Americans had been abused by President Nixon, who falsely and cynically claimed a national security justification for illegal—and politically motivated—domestic wiretapping. Information also surfaced in the mid-1970s that overzealous federal agencies had encroached on Americans' constitutionally based freedoms by engaging in extensive domestic surveillance, particularly of civil rights and antiwar activists.

Congress wanted to put an end to these abuses and stepped forward to create a system to meet national security needs, while protecting basic freedoms, including guarantees of the Fourth Amendment of the Bill of Rights.

In the late 1960s and early 1970s, the U.S. Supreme Court issued several decisions on the Fourth Amendment and wiretapping. The Fourth Amendment grew out of grievous experiences before the Revolutionary War when the British government broke into people's homes at will and gives Americans the right "to be secure in their persons, houses, papers, and effects" from "unreasonable searches and seizures." A protection against government abuse, the amendment states that searches are to be conducted only with a warrant and a showing of probable cause.(See Appendix D.) In 1967, the high court ruled that, under the Fourth Amendment, domestic wiretapping could not be conducted without a warrant. In a 1972 decision, the Supreme Court stated that even when domestic surveillance is conducted for national security purposes, court approval is still required.

These rulings motivated the administrations of both President Ford and President Carter to join with Congress to establish a comprehensive framework for lawful wiretapping of international terrorists and foreign agents.

Striking a careful balance in FISA, Congress reconciled the legitimate requirements of national security with protection against presidential or agency abuses and safeguards for the personal privacy of Americans. FISA used a simple device: wiretapping would have to be approved by a specially created court. Congress rejected entirely wiretapping on presidential say-so alone. Federal judges with lifetime tenure, sitting in terms on the FISA court, could say no to a president if surveillance requests were wrapped in national security but degenerated into domestic spying or other unconstitutional purposes.

The judges on the FISA court, selected by the chief justice of the Supreme Court, develop expertise in foreign intelligence issues, facilitating the quick and knowledgeable processing of surveillance applications ("FISA warrants"). The small number of judges on the court reduces the possibility of leaks—and there has never been any reported leak from the

FISA court. Files and cases are sealed and are not revealed, even when prosecutions result.

FISA warrants may be granted to allow physical and electronic surveillance of foreign powers, foreign agents, or international terrorists. The surveillance need only serve an intelligence purpose, that is, the collection of foreign intelligence or counterintelligence; no crime need be suspected. If the "target" is a U.S. person (U.S. citizen or permanent resident), the government must meet a higher standard before permission is granted. It must show that the surveillance is necessary to protect national defense or that there is probable cause to believe that the person's activities involve espionage or criminal conduct.

Proceedings of the FISA court are secret, but court reports indicate that it has granted approximately 19,000 surveillance warrants since its founding in 1979, and rejected only five. In 2005, it granted a record number of 2,072 applications and denied none. The FISA court clearly poses no obstacle to justified wiretaps. If anything, civil liberties groups believe that the FISA court grants too many government wiretap requests. Still, as I know from wiretap applications that my office brought when I served as the district attorney in Brooklyn in the 1980s, the independent review by a court stands as a barrier to abuse. The mere presence of the FISA court discourages the government from seeking warrants that are politically motivated, overly zealous, or otherwise improper.

In enacting FISA, Congress also understood that emergency situations arise when time does not allow for a warrant application. In such cases, court approval may be retroactive—initially within 24 hours, but amended in 2002 to 72 hours. Similarly, when Congress declares war, the need for court approval is suspended for 15 days, enough time to allow the president to determine whether FISA needs to be amended to meet special wartime conditions. The provision shows the thoroughness with which Congress approached various contingencies, and yet how insistent it remained on strict limitations on warrantless wiretapping by the president, even in wartime.

With the comprehensive framework in place, Congress stated that FISA was the "exclusive" method for undertaking foreign intelligence wiretapping in the United States. In passing the law, Congress explicitly rejected arguments of "inherent" presidential authority to conduct foreign surveillance intelligence and extinguished any "inherent authority" claim of the president to wiretap under any other law.

President Carter, in signing the FISA legislation, said the law "clarifies the Executive's authority to gather foreign intelligence by electronic surveillance in the United States. . . . It will assure FBI field agents and others involved in intelligence collection that their acts are authorized by statute and, if a U.S. person's communications are concerned, by a court order. And it will protect the privacy of the American people."

Of course, Congress knew that the law, which is of critical importance to our national security, would need to accommodate technological changes and new developments. The FISA law has been amended at least six times since its passage, according to the Center for National Security Studies. One amendment permits physical entries in connection with foreign intelligence surveillance; another allows trap/pen registers that, like caller ID boxes, record telephone numbers. Other modifications to the law were made by the U.S. Patriot Act.

In any case, after FISA was enacted, every president was obliged to comply with its terms or go back to Congress to seek adjustments. For twenty-three years, presidents successfully implemented the FISA law without apparent difficulties.

VIOLATION OF THE LAW ON CONDUCTING FOREIGN SURVEILLANCE

President Bush has not complied with the terms of FISA. The president decided, unilaterally, to override the law, and authorized others in the government to ignore its requirements. The president has allowed the National Security Agency (NSA), a government spy agency larger than the CIA, to conduct surveillance of U.S. citizens without a warrant and without court approval.

A great many details of President Bush's domestic spying program are still unknown because the program has been hidden from the public and most of Congress, and the president has refused to give clear and direct answers about it.

There actually seem to be at least two domestic spying programs; what else exists remains to be discovered. The first program—exposed by the *New York Times* on December 16, 2005—is apparently an eavesdropping program by which the

NSA listens in on telephone conversations between people in the United States and people in other countries; it may also include wiretapping of purely domestic conversations. An e-mail component may be part of the program, too.

While the public was still trying to understand the dimensions and extent of this program in the face of stonewalling by President Bush, a second program was exposed in *USA Today* on May 11, 2006. Under it, the NSA gained access to call identification records, or phone logs, indicating what calls have been made and received on the telephones and cell phones of tens of millions people in the United States.

The president authorized both of these secret surveillance programs—he has stated so publicly. The possibility exists that other programs, still unknown to the public, are underway.

The only monitoring of the programs is done by NSA employees. They operate the program, decide whom to monitor, what information to collect and keep, and how the information will be used. There is no congressional or judicial oversight.

Surveillance Program One: Intercepting Phone and E-mail Conversations without Court Approval

The eavesdropping program first exposed by the *New York Times* in December 2005 had been authorized by the president at least thirty times (for a forty-five-day period each time) since October 2001. We do not know who has been wiretapped under Bush's program and why, nor do we know how many people have been wiretapped. Attorney General Alberto Gonzales said that one of the persons must be outside the United States and "is somehow affiliated with al Qaeda." General Michael Hayden, the former director of the NSA who has since been appointed as CIA director, said the targets are "those associated with people who want to kill Americans."

We do not know, if, like President Nixon, President Bush has been wiretapping political opponents, antiwar activists, critics, journalists, lawyers who represent persons accusing the government of illegal detention, or others whom the administration may find desirable to target.

We also know virtually nothing about the utility of the program. Press reports suggest that "torrents" of leads from the wiretapping program were given to the FBI to follow up, but virtually all turned up negative. FBI agents reportedly thought the program "diverted" them from more productive counterterrorism work. The president claims that the wiretapping program uncovered a plot to destroy the Brooklyn Bridge and one to ignite a fertilizer bomb in London, but those claims have been vigorously disputed by FBI officials here and by British officials abroad.

Two interruptions occurred in the operation of the NSA surveillance programs. The first happened when Deputy Attorney General James Comey refused to sign off on the reauthorization of the NSA wiretapping program in 2004 while Attorney General Ashcroft was hospitalized. The reasons are unknown.

Another hitch arose from the FISA court itself. Reports indicate that Judge Colleen Kollar-Kotelly expressed concerns in 2003, and the program was temporarily suspended. After Bush's actions were disclosed in late 2005, one judge resigned, reportedly in protest.

For four years, the White House tried to hide its illicit and covert operations from the public and from Congress.

Once the wiretapping program was exposed, the president made a series of specious and completely unsatisfactory claims, attempting to justify the program. If anything, the faux justifications offered by the president, attorney general, and the Justice Department indicate the extent to which the White House knows how unlawful and unconstitutional the program is.

Surveillance Program Two: Domestic Call Tracking of Millions of Americans

Revelations in May 2006 disclosed an entirely different domestic surveillance program authorized by President Bush. Under this second secret program, the National Security Agency is obtaining tracking records of telephone calls made in the United States by tens of millions of Americans. The government said that the program was an effort to track terrorists.

According to *USA Today*, which first published the story, the NSA is building a massive database of every call, domestic or otherwise, made within the United States. The database is apparently one of the largest in the country.

Reportedly the program does not seek the content of phone calls, but the telephone numbers that were dialed—phone logs or call-detail records. Once the program was exposed, the government said that no personal identifiers are attached to the information, such as name, address, and credit card information, although a good deal of this information might be available from other databases.

NSA apparently purchased these records from the large telephone companies that handle billions of calls each year in the United States. AT&T, Inc. has not denied that it participated in the program, although BellSouth Corp. and Verizon, originally named by the newspaper as participants, issued qualified denials of participation. One telephone company, Qwest, said it refused to participate unless NSA secured approval from the FISA court. NSA declined to do so, undoubtedly recognizing this program would not meet FISA standards.

The program has not had the appproval of Congress, nor it seems, of any court.

Under FISA, when the government seeks to conduct foreign intelligence surveillance using a pen register—a method of tracking the phone calls of a particular person—certain standards must be met. The U.S. government must, at a minimum, show a foreign intelligence or counterintelligence purpose. This minimal standard could not be met with respect to most Americans.

Many unknowns are associated with this call-tracking program. It is not known what information is retained, or who oversees the program. Also unknown is if other "data-mining" of financial, voting, transportation, school, social security, employment, and health records is underway and if the information is being interconnected. Public alarm arose, even in a post-9/11 era, when the Pentagon's "Total Information Awareness" (TIA) project was first described in newspaper articles in November 2002. TIA planned to develop data-mining tools to integrate multiple public, private, and commercial databases into a "virtual, centralized, grand database," which it said would help track terrorists and provide law enforcement access to private data without the necessity of a warrant. Faced with an avalanche of public criticism, Congress cut off funding for TIA in September 2003. But the Electronic Privacy Information Center, a nonprofit advocacy group in Washington, D.C., wrote, "This does not, however, necessarily signal the end of other government date-mining initiatives."

Is the NSA now doing in secret what Congress and the public rejected? No one knows. Plainly, most people who make or receive telephone calls in the United States have nothing to do with terrorism, al Qaeda, or espionage. Many questions arise as to the constitutionality, legality, authority, and appropriateness of this domestic surveillance program.

IMPEACHABLE OFFENSES IN VIOLATING THE LAW ON FOREIGN INTELLIGENCE SURVEILLANCE

Nixon's authorization of illegal wiretaps of seventeen journalists and White House staffers formed one of the grounds for his impeachment.

As with President Bush, President Nixon's illegal wiretapping arose out of military hostilities. President Nixon was looking for the source of a 1969 newspaper leak about his secret bombing of Cambodia. The Nixon wiretaps quickly degenerated into political espionage: One of the White House staffers who was illegally wiretapped left and went to work for Senator Edmond Muskie, a candidate for president against Nixon. The wiretap conveniently gave President Nixon and his team a pipeline into an opponent's campaign.

A bipartisan majority of the House Judiciary Committee during Watergate found President Nixon's illegal wiretapping program constituted a serious abuse of power and an impeachable offense.

President's Bush's failure to obey the FISA statute violates his duty to take care that the laws are faithfully executed. It contravenes his oath of office, which requires him to obey the laws, and uphold the Constitution. Violation of the law is clearly a basis for impeachment.

The president could seek to amend or rewrite or repeal the FISA law. As noted, he has said that he will not.

President Bush has repeatedly deceived the American people about his wiretaps.

No president is above the law. That was a bitter lesson driven home in Watergate. President Bush's conduct is a vast and grave abuse of power. In addition to violating the basic rights of an untold number of Americans, it is a breathtaking defiance of the federal law and our constitutional scheme of government. These actions constitute high crimes and misdemeanors.

EVIDENCE OF PRESIDENTIAL ACTS IN ILLEGALLY CONDUCTING DOMESTIC WIRETAPPING

The president admits that he has not adhered to the federal law prohibiting him from conducting electronic surveillance without seeking a court order. While he conducted these activities secretly for years, he now asserts a number of justifications for them. If those justifications fall away, plainly he stands as a lawbreaker. None of the justifications is valid.

His arguments have been discredited by a variety of legal analysts. Fourteen distinguished law professors, law school deans, and lawyers (including a former judge and director of the FBI) wrote to key House and Senate members on January 9, 2006, that the president's domestic wiretapping program "appears on its face to violate existing law." The Justice Department, they said, has "failed to offer a plausible legal defense" for the domestic spying program.

The initial justification by the president for refusing to comply with FISA was frivolous. When the wiretapping program was first disclosed in December 2005, both the president and his attorney general blamed cumbersome procedures for their disregard of FISA. FISA took too much time, and the country, they argued, had to be nimble in fighting al Qaeda.

But President Bush and Attorney General Gonzales seem to have been caught off guard, because, as was noted, emergency wiretaps may be commenced under FISA without any warrant, and court approval obtained later. Clearly, concerns over slow response could not have been the cause for violating FISA. Not surprisingly, the "speed" argument drifted away.

What is the real reason that the president believes that he is entitled to ignore the law? The president's "legal justification has evolved over time," Attorney General Gonzales wrote in a letter to Senator Arlen Specter, chair of the Senate Judiciary Committee, on February 28, 2006. This language gives the clear impression that some of the justifications might have been developed along the way, after-the-fact rationalizations for a program that was never supposed to see the light of day.

President Bush's two central arguments for his right to break the FISA law are that Congress authorized him to violate the law, and that it is his right, as commander in chief, to violate the law. Both are wrong.

THE PRESIDENT CANNOT CLAIM THAT CONGRESS AUTHORIZED HIM TO CONDUCT ILLEGAL SURVEILLANCE

The president's main defense of his domestic surveillance scheme is skimpy—and incorrect.

He claims that Congress authorized him to conduct warrantless domestic surveillance, even though Congress is and was utterly unaware of this and disagrees. The president said that when the Congress passed the Authorization for Use of Military Force (AUMF), the so-called "force resolution", in September 2001, permitting the president to commence military hostilities against al Qaeda in Afghanistan after 9/11, Congress also authorized the president to ignore FISA and conduct warrantless wiretapping.

This claim represents an audacious grab—and abuse—of power by the executive branch.

For multiple reasons, it has no merit:

- Nothing whatsoever in the force resolution mentions wiretapping, overriding FISA, or allowing the president to wiretap without court approval.
- Members of Congress did not believe they were overriding FISA. Senator Lindsay Graham, a conservative Republican, has said that he didn't think he was voting to override FISA when he voted for the force resolution. He said he "never envisioned that the AUMF would give the president carte blanche to go around FISA."
- Given how controversial wiretapping is because of its highly intrusive quality, Congress surely would have debated the subject if there had been any inkling that the force resolution was designed to override FISA. But there was not one word of debate about it.
- Former Senator Tom Daschle has stated that before the passage of the force resolution, the administration tried to add language permitting its use for activities "inside the

United States." That effort was flatly rebuffed. The administration would not have sought the amendment if it believed that the force resolution allowed it to operate a domestic spying program. At that time, Daschle was the majority leader and negotiated these issues with the Bush administration.

- Because the FISA statutory scheme is so comprehensive and specific, another statute would not be viewed as over-ruling FISA without some explicit language to that effect. There is none in the force resolution.

The president has no basis whatsoever to claim that he was granted the right to conduct surveillance in the United States based on the authorization to use military force.

The president also said that the wiretaps are justified because he told a handful of members of the House of Representatives and the Senate about it—perhaps eight out of 535.

The comprehensiveness of the briefings is unclear. Not much is known about them because of extensive constraints placed on participants. They could not take notes, nor could they discuss the matter with their staffs, which meant that they could not explore the program in the depth it deserved. Despite these obstacles, at least two members of the group— Senator Jay Rockefeller and House Minority Leader Nancy Pelosi—expressed their reservations at the time.

In defending the vast call-tracking program, the president said that "appropriate" members of Congress were briefed, but Pelosi responded that the administration refused to provide details about who was briefed and when.

Briefing eight members of Congress, or "appropriate" members of Congress, is not the equivalent of congressional approval and may not amend a law.

In using these members of Congress as a foil for his illegal wiretapping, the president may have also violated his responsibilities to keep the House and Senate Intelligence Committees—as a whole—informed of his activities. These committees were not apprised of the program. The National Security Act requires just that, however: House and Senate Intelligence Committees are to be "fully and currently informed of the intelligence activities of the United States."

THE PRESIDENT CANNOT CLAIM THAT HE MAY IGNORE FISA BECAUSE HE IS COMMANDER IN CHIEF

The president's most dangerous claim in support of his domestic surveillance program is that he is the commander in chief and so he can override any congressional statute purporting to limit his powers when it comes to national security.

The president's view is profoundly wrong.

The founders of our republic feared unlimited executive power, just as they opposed all unlimited governmental power. In preventing the accumulation of unlimited powers, the system of checks and balances protects the freedoms of Americans.

President Carter protected the very same freedoms when he signed the FISA bill. He and Congress acted in their most important capacities—as protectors of the Bill of Rights, as well as protectors of the nation's security.

In violating FISA, President Bush showed not only contempt for Congress, the FISA court, and the concept of separation of powers contained in the Constitution, but also for the Fourth Amendment freedom that FISA seeks to safeguard. No court has ever ruled that a president has the power to violate a federal law, if it is constitutional, whether in his capacity as commander in chief or otherwise.

In 1952, the Supreme Court considered the powers of a war president during the Korean conflict when President Harry Truman issued an order seizing the steel mills to forestall a strike. The president argued that steel was critical to the war effort and that he was acting within his power as commander in chief. The Supreme Court rejected the claim in the case of *Youngstown Sheet & Tube Co.* v. *Sawyer.* Justice Jackson, in a famous opinion, said the president's powers as commander in chief are "subject to limitations consistent with a constitutional Republic whose law and policymaking branch is a representative Congress." (See Appendix G.) The president's command power is at its "lowest ebb," he said, when Congress has acted on an issue. That is the case with foreign intelligence surveillance. Congress, after all, enacted FISA and has a central responsibility to "provide for the common defense."

Justice Jackson, who had previously served as the chief prosecutor at the Nuremberg trials, was emphatic. The president has "no monopoly of 'war powers,'" he wrote, and, Jackson underscored, the president is commander in chief of the army and the navy; he is not "Commander in Chief of the country."

In February 2006, Senator Graham, a conservative and former judge advocate in the military, made a similar point. "When a nation is at war, you need checks and balances more than ever," he said.

If the president is permitted to break the law on wiretapping, then a president can break any other law. It is a formula for dictatorship. To allow the president, through his role as commander in chief, to follow or break laws as he sees fit, adds only one word to that sentence: it is a formula for a military dictatorship.

The systems of checks and balances do not vanish in wartime. The president's role as commander in chief does not swallow up Congress's powers, and does not wipe out the Bill of Rights. As U.S. Supreme Court Justice Sandra Day O'Connor wrote, "a state of war is not a blank check for the president when it comes to the rights of the nation's citizens."

PRESIDENTIAL REFUSAL TO SEEK CONGRESSIONAL AMENDMENTS OR ADJUSTMENTS

President Bush has refused to seek an amendment to the FISA law to accommodate his wiretapping program, although members of Congress have invited him to do so.

Presidents frequently seek to amend or repeal laws with which they disagree. President Reagan had no problem amending a provision that I had championed in Congress.

Representative John Burton and I had won passage of a law that said the United States could not commence any covert activity "unless and until" a report had been made to Congress. Then President Reagan came into office, and he objected to the law. But instead of ignoring it, he went to Congress and got it repealed.

President Bush has refused to advise the Congress of new post 9/11 facts that call for adjustments to the FISA law. One excuse offered by his administration is that pursuing amendments would reveal the wiretapping program's details and undermine its effectiveness. This argument is a red herring. Congress has extensive procedures for considering classified material and has done so in the past.

On the other hand, the president may have declined to seek amendments because Congress, even a congress dominated by his own party, would have rejected his proposals. In a press briefing on December 19, 2005, after the program became publicly known, Attorney General Alberto Gonzales said, "We have had discussions with Congress in the past—certain members of Congress—as to whether or not FISA could be amended to allow us to adequately deal with this kind of threat, and we were advised that that would be difficult, if not impossible." Congressional approval, he said, "was not something we could likely get."

If this is the reception that Bush's wartime surveillance proposals received from a Congress dominated by members of his own party, the wiretapping program must be extraordinarily invasive and constitutionally suspect.

The president is wholly capable of getting Congress to accept reasonable amendments to FISA—the law has been modified several times on his watch. He sought and secured an extension for retroactive court approvals of emergency surveillance from twenty-four hours to seventy-two hours. So there is no excuse for his defiance of the law. In any case, the president must still obey the law, whether he likes its provisions or not.

PRESIDENTIAL COVER-UP AND DECEPTIONS ABOUT THE WARRANTLESS WIRETAP PROGRAM

Prior to the disclosure of the domestic spying program in the *New York Times*, President Bush took active steps to deceive the American people about his use of warrantless and judicially unapproved wiretaps. This cover-up and the extent of these lies are a breach of trust with the American people, and add to the web of impeachable offenses emerging from the illegal surveillance of American citizens.

Two and a half years after the NSA warrantless wiretapping program began, President Bush stated in an April 20, 2004, speech in Buffalo: "Now, by the way, any time you hear the United States government talking about wiretap, it requires—a wiretap requires a court order. Nothing has changed by the way. When we're talking about chasing down terrorists, we're talking about getting a court order before we do so."

A few months later, on July 14, 2004, in Wisconsin, President Bush said, "Any action that takes place by law enforcement requires a court order. In other words, the government can't move on wiretaps or roving wiretaps without getting a court order."

A year later, in Columbus, Ohio, on June 9, 2005, President Bush stated, "Law enforcement officers need a federal judge's permission to wiretap a foreign terrorist's phone, a federal judge's permission to track his calls, or a federal judge's permission to search his property. Officers must meet strict standards to use any of these tools. And these standards are fully consistent with the Constitution of the U.S."

In each of these instances, President Bush knew that he was not telling the truth. At the time each of those statements was made, President Bush had personally authorized, and was continuing to authorize, wiretaps without warrants, without judicial approval, without a court order. But for his own political advantage, he affirmatively deceived the American people. The first two instances occurred in an election year during a difficult election campaign; the third arose as he was trying to obtain reauthorization of the Patriot Act. Telling the truth might have caused him to lose support.

There may have been other reasons for lying to the public. Violation of FISA is a crime. President Bush's conduct may not only be impeachable, but criminal.

In President Nixon's case, repeated and insistent lying to the American people formed one of the grounds for impeachment, and it was supported by a majority of the House Judiciary Committee. A few months after the Watergate break-in, President Nixon told the American people that his White House counsel had "conducted a complete investigation of all leads which

might involve any present members of the White House staff."
He reported on its conclusions. "I can say categorically that
[the] investigation indicates that no one in the White House . . .
was involved in this very bizarre incident," Nixon said.
Problem is, there was no such investigation, no report, and
the president knew White House staffers had been directly
involved. President Bush's untruthful statements to the public
that concealed illegal activities may form the grounds for
impeachment, just as President Nixon's statements did.

Once the warrantless wiretapping program by President Bush
was uncovered and the White House learned that an article was
to appear in the *New York Times*, the president tried to convince
the paper not to publish it. When the story ran anyhow, the
president told the American people that he had done nothing
wrong, that he had committed no crime and violated no constitutional safeguard against illegal government searches. But he
did so based on misleading and deceptive claims.

In his State of the Union address before Congress and the
American people on January 31, 2006, President Bush sought
to justify his illegal wiretapping. He avoided mentioning the
sole issue at stake: whether he was required to seek FISA court
approval for the wiretaps of Americans. He offered no explana-
tion for his refusal to seek court approval. He simply said, "Previous Presidents have used the same constitutional authority I
have and federal courts have approved the use of that authority."

That claim is untrue. No court has ruled that a president
can override the FISA framework, according to a January 5,
2006, memorandum of the Congressional Research Service.

When Attorney General Gonzales was asked at a Senate hearing on February 6, 2006, to provide an example of any other governmental wiretapping that did not adhere to FISA since it was enacted in 1978, he could not.

One of those former presidents, President Jimmy Carter, told reporters on February 6, 2006, that President Bush has broken the law. "Under the Bush administration, there's been a disgraceful and illegal decision—we're not going to let the judges or the Congress or anyone else know that we're spying on the American people," Carter said. "And no one knows how many innocent Americans have had their privacy violated under this secret act."

Admiral Bobby Ray Inman, former NSA director under Carter, also criticized President Bush at a forum in New York on May 8, 2006, challenging Bush either to change the law governing wiretapping or abandon the wiretapping program. "The activity is not authorized," said Inman.

After the warrantless domestic wiretapping was disclosed in December 2005, the president said that domestic surveillance was carefully targeted to include only international calls and those that involve suspected al Qaeda operatives or associates. This was not true. In May 2006, a vast government program was exposed that tracks the called numbers of millions of people in the United States who have no association with al Qaeda.

The president's effort to persuade the people of the legality of his warrantless wiretaps is based on a series of ongoing falsehoods and key omissions that betray the trust that the American people have placed in him.

POTENTIAL OFFENSES IN THE AUTHORIZATION OF BREAK-INS AND DOMESTIC SURVEILLANCE WITHOUT A WARRANT

President Bush claims he has the inherent power as commander in chief to engage in warrantless wiretaps for foreign intelligence purposes in violation of FISA. Does he similarly claim he has the power to break into people's homes without a warrant in violation of FISA, or engage in purely domestic wiretapping that has no foreign surveillance component?

Break-ins may very well be in the mix. During the hearings before the Senate Judiciary Committee on warrantless wiretaps on February 6, 2006, senators repeatedly asked Attorney General Gonzales whether the president's warrantless surveillance program contemplated break-ins and other illegal activities. The attorney general avoided answering; plainly, he could have said "no." His evasion leaves open the possibility that such activities are ongoing.

Later, information emerged showing that the president also authorized the collection of telephone call numbers of millions of people in the United States without court approval or congressional authorization. On May 11, 2006, the president said, "We're not mining or trolling through the personal lives of millions of innocent Americans." But he has refused to provide any details that could permit any crosscheck of his blanket assertions.

In comments to the House Judiciary Committee on February 6, 2006, Attorney General Gonzales left the impression that the Bush surveillance programs could include domestic wiretapping without court approval. When asked whether the president might order wholly domestic spying without a warrant, Gonzales responded, "I'm not going to rule it out."

If the president is ignoring court approval and warrant requirements in all these situations, we are witnessing a wholesale attack on the Fourth Amendment and on our constitutional system of government.

During Watergate, one of the grounds for the impeachment of Richard Nixon was his approval of the Huston plan. This plan was developed against the huge groundswell of anti–Vietnam War protests. In order to get "actionable intelligence," the Nixon administration created a program for collecting information that included breaking into people's homes and wiretapping illegally.

President Bush's plan replicates Nixon's, insofar as warrantless eavesdropping is concerned. Based on what the attorney general has told us, other parts of the Huston plan may have been revived, as well. Congress, an independent commission or a special prosecutor, needs to inquire and demand answers. If the answers point to purely domestic wiretapping, break-ins, and other illegal surveillance activities of Americans, impeachment on these grounds surely is in order.

POTENTIAL OFFENSES IN THE PRESIDENT'S DOMESTIC CALL-TRACKING PROGRAM

The second secret domestic surveillance program of the NSA, tracking the calls of tens of millions of Americans, is one of staggering proportions. Many questions arise about it: Does the NSA's vast call surveillance program violate constitutional privacy rights? May the NSA keep private phone call records without strict standards on their use? Is the NSA also capturing e-mail, and if so, is content or partial content collected? May the NSA purchase records from private companies without approval from Congress or individual account owners?

The president asserted that the program is legal. But what is his legal justification for it? If the program is legal, why was it not shared with Congress or approval sought from the FISA court?

The president's adoption of a vast domestic surveillance program without the approval of Congress or the courts and without strict guidelines on the use of the information is chilling and troubling. With further inquiries into the details of this program, potential violations of the law by the president may emerge, and the secret call-tracking program may be added to the list of impeachable offenses of President Bush.

CONCLUSION: WHY IMPEACHMENT IS NECESSARY FOR THE PRESIDENT'S ILLEGAL WIRETAPPING

The president has not denied that he has secretly authorized wiretapping prohibited by law for several years. Instead, he has asserted, "I have the authority, both from the Constitution and the Congress."

The president also has not denied that he authorized a second secret program to track phones calls made by millions of Americans. He claims it is in his power to do so, without judicial oversight or congressional approval.

Both the warrantless domestic wiretapping program and the massive domestic call-tracking program may have much more to do with restoring the trappings of the imperial presidency than they have to do with protecting the nation's security.

The president's approval of a domestic spying program without court approval, his threats to continue it for as long as he sees fit, his effort to cover up the illegality of his actions with spurious legal contentions, his creation of a second program tracking the calls of Americans, all combine to create a clear and present danger to the rule of law.

In this instance, impeachment is not simply a way of punishing the president for past misconduct. Impeachment is also a way to protect America against his continuing violation of our laws and infringement of our basic liberties.

With these illegal surveillance programs, President Bush has, in essence, said I can ignore the law at will; stop me if you can. There is no constitutional method for stopping the president's unlawful behavior other than impeachment and removal from office.

CHAPTER FIVE

Impeachment for Permitting Torture

OVERVIEW

The images that poured across on television and Web sites in April 2004 left indelible impressions: a man, stripped of his clothing, kneeling with a leash around his collar; a hooded figure, standing on a box, arms stretched and wires dangling from his fingers; a fierce guard dog baring its teeth at man in an orange jump suit, cowering; a pyramid of naked men arranged in a sexually suggestive pose. Nearly as painful as the pictures of prisoners at Abu Ghraib in Iraq was the sight of those in charge, guards in U.S. uniforms, many smiling.

After the Abu Ghraib photographs were released, I read a collection of writings by Vasily Grossman, a Russian journalist who traveled to the Treblinka concentration camp at the end of World War II and interviewed survivors. He described the Nazi policy of forcing the Jews to remove all their clothes before going into the gas chambers. "We know from the cruel reality of recent years that a naked person immediately loses the strength to resist, to struggle against his fate. When stripped, a person immediately loses the strength of the instinct to live and one accepts one's destiny like a fate," he wrote. Grossman's language stirred an awful association.

The Abu Ghraib pictures offered a ghastly view of U.S. interrogation methods. The revelations stunned Americans and the world. Torture is wrong: it has been condemned worldwide and is the tool of repressive regimes and power-thirsty dictators. Many Americans expressed shame.

These revelations also harmed the United States. Even President Bush has acknowledged this. Pictures from Abu Ghraib intensified anti-American feeling around the world and increased the danger to U.S. troops by inciting jihadis and guerrillas to fight the United States.

The president and Secretary of Defense Rumsfeld tried to minimize the scope of the abuse by placing the blame on iso-lated low-level personnel—"the actions of a few bad apples," in the words of White House spokesperson Trent Duffy. But investigations by groups both inside and outside the govern-ment point to systematic and widespread problems.

The original act that set these problems in motion traces to President Bush. The president unilaterally voided, or attempted to void, obligations under U.S. and international laws that ban torture and cruel, inhuman, or degrading treatment of prisoners.

His act unleashed aggressive interrogations by U.S. personnel that led to the abuses in Abu Ghraib and elsewhere. The refusal by the president to "faithfully execute" the laws that prohibit torture or brutal mistreatment of detainees is an impeachable offense, as is his failure to demand a full investigation of all those who may have contributed to it—whether they are military or civilian, no matter their rank or position.

ACTS OF TORTURE BY U.S. PERSONNEL

The Department of Defense has conducted approximately eight hundred investigations of prisoner abuse at the hands of U.S. personnel in Iraq and Afghanistan, according to a May 2006 report by U.S. officials to the UN Committee against Torture in Geneva. Other complaints have been raised by detainees held by the United States at the specially built prison camp at the U.S. Naval base in Guantanamo Bay, Cuba, or "Gitmo." It is not unlikely that other stories of mistreatment will emerge.

Major General Antonio Taguba, who investigated abuses at Abu Ghraib, released a report in February 2004 that describes "numerous incidents of sadistic, blatant, and wanton criminal abuses . . . inflicted on several detainees." He called it "systemic and illegal abuse of detainees" that was "intentionally perpetrated" and included acts of "punching, slapping and kicking detainees," rape, use of military dogs to intimidate detainees, and other types of mistreatment.

The watchdog and advocacy organization Human Rights First reported in February 2006 that nearly 100 detainees had died in U.S. custody since August 2002, including 45 cases of suspected or confirmed homicides that were the result of physical abuse or harsh conditions of detention. The U.S. delegation to the Committee against Torture in Geneva reported in May 2006 that 29 detainees died in U.S. facilities in Iraq and Afghanistan of what appeared to be abuse or other violations of U.S. law.

Other issues of inhuman and illegal treatment are raised by three covert CIA programs—rendition, secret prisons, and "ghost" detainees. These programs violate U.S. and international laws.

"Rendition" or "extraordinary rendition" occurs when the CIA delivers prisoners to other countries, such as Morocco, Egypt, or Jordan, where their treatment is likely to be abusive. More than seventy renditions of detainees have occurred since 2001, according to an article by Dana Priest in the *Washington Post* on November 2, 2005. Attorney General Gonzales has admitted that detainees have been turned over to other countries.

In other cases, the CIA has taken high-level al Qaeda detainees to secret CIA-run prisons in other countries, according to Priest. Priest further stated that approximately thirty U.S. detainees are in these "black sites," believed initially to be in Eastern European countries. The United States has refused to comment on black sites.

The CIA and military personnel also have held "ghost detainees" in U.S. facilities—people who are kept in isolation and are not on the official prison register. According to a

March 11, 2005, article by *Washington Post* writer Josh White, as many as one hundred ghost detainees are held in prisons in Iraq. Secretary of Defense Rumsfeld has admitted the existence of ghost detainees.

Several investigations of the mistreatment have been conducted. All, however, have been limited in their scope. As a result, the roles of the CIA and upper level personnel, including the president, the vice president, and the secretary of defense, have not been scrutinized.

BACKGROUND: PROHIBITIONS ON TORTURE

The Geneva Conventions of 1949 were developed in response to the horrific mistreatment of civilians and prisoners of war in World War II. They enhanced earlier versions that dated to the Hague Conventions of 1907 and the first international humanitarian rules for wartime, adopted in 1864. After World War II, many Americans still carried raw memories of the abysmal treatment of U.S. prisoners of war by the Japanese and viewed protecting future U.S. POWs from torture or abuse as a matter of great importance. General Douglas MacArthur, no bleeding heart, deemed the Geneva Conventions vital to the safety and protection of U.S. troops, announcing at the outset of the Korean conflict that he would voluntarily abide by them, even though they had not yet been ratified by the United States.

The U.S. ratification came during the term of President Dwight D. Eisenhower, who also understood their importance from his experiences as allied commander during World

War II. "The Geneva Conventions are fashioned primarily to meet universal humanitarian aspirations and needs," President Eisenhower wrote. They are, he said, "for the relief of physical suffering and moral degradation so often in the past experienced by victims of war, both military and civilian." Once the U.S. ratification was completed in 1955, the Geneva Conventions became U.S. law. As Article VI of the U.S. Constitution notes: "All treaties made . . . under the Authority of the United States, shall be the supreme Law of the Land."

The Geneva Conventions require certain standards of treatment for prisoners of war and, separately, for civilians. In both cases, the Geneva Conventions prohibit "cruel treatment and torture" and "outrages upon personal dignity, in particular humiliating or degrading treatment." In addition, the Conventions prohibit what are termed "grave breaches"—or the "wilful killing, torture or inhuman treatment" and "wilfully causing great suffering or serious injury to body or health." (See Appendix H.)

Since they were ratified, the United States has observed the Geneva Conventions in every armed conflict. There is, said former Secretary of State Colin Powell in January 2002, "over a century of U.S. policy and practice in supporting the Geneva Conventions." The rules for interrogations contained in the U.S. *Army Field Manual for Intelligence Interrogations* fully comply with the Geneva Conventions and prohibit the "use of force, mental torture, threats, insults, or exposure to unpleasant and inhumane treatment of any kind." According to the *Field Manual,* torture is a poor technique that leads to unreliable results. Since many people confronted with physical and mental pain will say whatever they believe the interrogator wants to hear, the "intelligence" is rarely useful, the *Field Manual* notes. The U.S. government applied the Geneva Conventions during the Vietnam War to all captured parties, whether in uniform or guerrilla fighters.

By contrast, the North Vietnamese rejected the application of the Geneva Conventions, which they had ratified, and subjected U.S. troops to vicious, degrading treatment and torture. They said that Geneva Conventions did not apply because there had been no formal declaration of war between North Vietnam and the United States, and U.S. detainees were "criminals" not entitled to prisoner-of-war treatment. But there is no such loophole: the Geneva Conventions do not require a formal declaration of war and make no such exception.

In 1996, the United States strengthened its observance of the Geneva Convention by adopting the War Crimes Act of 1996. U.S. Rep. Walter B. Jones Jr., a Republican from North Carolina whose district included a naval station, an air force base, and Camp Lejeune, introduced the legislation. Because of his interest in protecting military personnel, he heeded the plea for more U.S. enforcement of war crime violations by a former U.S. pilot in Vietnam who had been held as a prisoner of war in brutal conditions for six years. Liberal and conservative members of Congress joined to pass the War Crimes Act, and President Bill Clinton signed it into law on August 21, 1996.

Under the War Crimes Act, war criminals can be prosecuted directly in the United States. The commission of any act that qualifies as a "grave breach" under the Geneva Conventions is a felony. If an act causes death, the perpetrator can be subjected to the death penalty. There is no statute of limitations in death cases.

The United States has other treaty and legal obligations that proscribe torture.

The Convention against Torture and Other Cruel, Inhuman or Degrading Treatment or Punishment, adopted by the UN in 1984, was ratified by United States in 1994. It prohibits the intentional infliction of "severe pain or suffering, whether physical or mental" upon a person in custody. Public officials are obliged to prevent torture and to intervene if they become aware of it. There are "no exceptional circumstances" to justify torture, including a state of war. When President Ronald Reagan sent the Convention against Torture to Congress for ratification, he wrote that it will "clearly express United States opposition to torture, an abhorrent practice unfortunately still prevalent in the world today."

An antitorture law enacted in 1994 is based on the Convention against Torture and makes torture a federal crime. (Sections 2340-2340A of the U.S. Criminal Code).

The U.S. Constitution also addresses torture in the Bill of Rights. The Eighth Amendment prohibits the use of cruel and unusual punishment. The Fifth Amendment bans the use of compelled testimony in a criminal prosecution, including information obtained by violence or abuse, a granite indictment of torture. (See Appendix D.)

At their core, the Geneva Conventions set a clear value that prizes the safety and welfare of captured troops in a time of war over any information that might be obtained from inhumane or degrading interrogations.

IMPEACHABLE OFFENSES OF PRESIDENT BUSH CONNECTED TO TORTURE

Under the Constitution, the president must take care to faithfully enforce the laws, including the War Crimes Act, the Geneva Conventions, and other prohibitions against torture. This, he did not do. His actions contravening these laws and treaties are serious abuses of power—high crimes or misdemeanors that call for impeachment.

The mistreatment of detainees was the foreseeable and direct consequence of actions by President Bush, who declared on February 7, 2002, that the Geneva Conventions did not apply to prisoners in Afghanistan and in Guantanamo. The president's objective in doing so was to allow harsh interrogation of detainees, despite the laws against it. The president failed to "take care" to "faithfully execute the laws." Instead he sought ways to circumvent the law, and to enable those who used torture to avoid punishment. This is an impeachable offense.

By pushing aside the laws that prevented military interrogators from using torture and cruel, inhuman, and degrading methods, the president opened the door to brutal interrogations and sent a signal that officials would turn a blind eye to them. The president also failed to set any limits on the CIA's treatment of detainees.

Rumsfeld approved aggressive interrogation techniques for use at Guantanamo detention center, techniques that eventually migrated to Iraq. In Iraq, the Geneva Conventions were clearly in force, and President Bush had an active duty to ensure that they were strictly followed. There is no evidence that he did this.

Once allegations of torture and cruel and degrading treatment came to the president's attention, he failed to demand a complete and thorough investigation, including military and civilian higher-ups and CIA officers, and to hold all wrongdoers accountable. These are obligations specifically imposed by law, but the president did not fulfill his obligations. His actions have had adverse consequences for the United States.

THE EVIDENCE OF PRESIDENTIAL ACTS PERMITTING OR CONDONING TORTURE

President Bush Lays the Track for U.S. Torture

On February 7, 2002, President Bush issued a two-page memorandum that shattered long-standing U.S. traditions about military interrogation techniques and broke with historic practices under the Geneva Conventions. At the same time, it violated the U.S. Constitution and statutes concerning torture and abuse of war detainees.

The memo applied to the war in Afghanistan, and addressed the treatment of al Qaeda members and the Taliban. No detainees from either group would be granted prisoner-of-war status, the president wrote. As a consequence, they would not be entitled to the protections of the Geneva Conventions, shielding them from "wilful killing, torture or inhuman treatment" and willfully caused "great suffering or serious injury to body or health."

Until President Bush issued this memo, the Geneva Conventions had been applied in every conflict. They provide specific rules on how war prisoners are to be treated and the conditions of their detention. (See Appendix H.) If any doubt existed about the status of a person captured in a conflict, a military tribunal convened to decide the matter, as the Geneva Conventions require. The State Department questioned the legality of the president's approach.

After disposing of the application of the Geneva Conventions, the president's memo continued in vague generalities that did not begin to approximate the specific and long-standing rules and legal practices developed under the Geneva Conventions. Members of the armed forces, he said, should treat detainees "humanely," although he offered no definition of what that meant. Even this hazy directive was undermined because, according to the memo, "military necessity" would take precedence, although it also was not defined. Strikingly, the CIA was omitted from even this fuzzy formulation.

The memo, published in *The Torture Papers* edited by Karen J. Greenberg and Joshua L. Dratel and in other publications, endorsed an "anything goes" attitude in interrogation. It was "vague and lacking," according to "The

Schlesinger Report" released by the Independent Panel to Review Department of Defense Detention Operations and its chair, former Defense Secretary James R. Schlesinger, in a later review of the torture scandals in Iraq.

The president's decision did spark opposition, both in the United States and around the world. The American Bar Association strongly criticized the president's view that anyone at all should be exempt from the protections of the Geneva Conventions, since a person is either a civilian—a person who has put down arms or has been captured—or is a prisoner of war. As with all other critics, the ABA was ignored.

By the time the president's memo was issued, four months had passed since the onset of the war in Afghanistan in October 2001. Detainees had been arriving at Guantanamo since January 11, 2002. The full story of possible mistreatment of detainees—both before February 7 and after—is yet to be uncovered.

The president's February 7 decision did have an impact. It led to or sanctioned mistreatment of prisoners held at Guantanamo Bay that was characterized as "tantamount to torture" by the International Committee of the Red Cross (ICRC). The president's decision also led to or sanctioned brutal treatment of prisoners at Bagram Air Base and elsewhere in Afghanistan.

As attention shifted from the war in Afghanistan, al Qaeda, and the Taliban to the decision to invade Iraq, the February 7 memo led, inevitably and inexorably, to the horrors of Abu Ghraib and other detention sites in Iraq.

The President Was on Notice of Criminal Violations Arising Out of Mistreatment of Detainees

The February 7 memorandum was issued by the president to avoid criminal liability under U.S. law for the abusers of detainees or their superiors or others who might have a guiding hand in the abuse—possibly even himself.

The president had been warned twice that the War Crimes Act of 1996 would apply to interrogations of detainees from Afghanistan if the Geneva Conventions applied. Gonzales sent a memo on January 25, 2002, and Attorney General John Ashcroft sent a letter on February 1, 2002.

The War Crimes Act imposes severe criminal penalties, including the death penalty, for violations of the Geneva Conventions. For this reason, the broad language of the Geneva Conventions troubled Gonzales. He advised President Bush that it would be impossible to predict whom future "special counsels" would prosecute. Since special counsels generally were picked to prosecute high-level officials, including presidents, Gonzales may have had the legal liability of President Bush himself in mind.

Ashcroft, too, indicated his deep concern about serious criminal liability under the War Crimes Act for law enforcement officials, intelligence officials, and military officials.

Why were they so anxious? Gonzales and Ashcroft had nothing to worry about if standard U.S. interrogation techniques were in effect. The *U.S. Army Field Manual* was carefully written to conform to the requirements of the Geneva Conventions. If U.S. personnel followed the precepts of Geneva, there could be no prosecutions under the War Crimes Act. Plainly, Gonzales and Ashcroft were nervous because the standard interrogation techniques either had been, or were about to be, abandoned.

There is no question that the president understood what he was doing. In his memo to the president, Gonzales references a conversation he had with the president on the same topic just a few days earlier—"As I discussed with you," he wrote.

In order to shield himself and others from future criminal prosecutions, the president undertook to nullify the War Crimes Act. Since the War Crimes Act takes its effect from the Geneva Conventions, the reasoning held that if the Geneva Conventions did not apply, then the War Crimes Act could not apply either.

President Bush had an obligation to enforce the War Crimes Act, not to gut it. He had an obligation to enforce the Geneva Conventions, not to circumvent them. But he chose otherwise. He sought to permit mistreatment, including possible torture of U.S. detainees, without criminal consequences to the individuals or higher ups involved.

If violations of the War Crimes Act had already occurred, his obligation under the Constitution was to ensure that these violations were investigated and prosecuted. If violations of the War Crimes Act were about to occur, his obligation was to prevent them from occurring. Instead, the president said crimes could take place with impunity, effectively authorizing and facilitating the mistreatment of U.S. detainees.

THE PRESIDENT'S SPECIAL OBLIGATIONS
TO PREVENT TORTURE IN IRAQ

Although the president limited the applicability of the Geneva Conventions when it came to the Afghan conflict, Iraq was a different story. He made it plain that the Geneva Conventions applied to the war in Iraq.

The president had a clear obligation to ensure that the interrogation methods used in Guantanamo and Afghanistan did not infiltrate and pollute interrogations in Iraq after the invasion there on March 19, 2003. He did nothing of the sort. The president's actions permitted brutal interrogations to migrate.

Several methods of interrogation in Guantanamo were approved for use by Rumsfeld that would not have been sanctioned under the Geneva Conventions. They included removal of clothing, use of hoods and dogs, isolation for long periods, stress positions, sleep, and light deprivation. "In so doing, [Rumsfeld] undercut long-standing prohibitions on the use of torture and other inhuman and degrading treatment," wrote Rear Admiral John D. Hutson, former Navy judge advocate general, and Brigadier General James Cullen, former judge advocate and chief judge of the Army's Court of Criminal Appeals in *Legal Times* in 2005. "Rumsfeld put in place policies that facilitated the disgraceful acts about which we read with numbing regularity."

On August 31, 2003, these techniques were flown to Iraq in the pocket of Army Major General Geoffrey D. Miller, the head of the detention facility at Guantanamo, who traveled there to conduct an assessment of counterterrorism interrogation and detention operations, according to the "The Schlesinger Report." He was to discuss how to "exploit internees rapidly for actionable intelligence." The exact origins of Miller's trip to Abu Ghraib are shrouded in mystery. In a May 21, 2004, article *Washington Post* journalist R. Jeffrey Smith said the order went to Miller in a memo signed on August 18, 2003, from "the Pentagon's Joint Staff—acting on a request from Rumsfeld and his top intelligence aide, Stephen A. Cambone."

The commander of the military police at Abu Ghraib, Brigadier General Janis Karpinski, said Miller told her that he was sent to "Gitmo-ize" interrogations of Iraqis. Whatever his exact motives or orders, it is undisputed that Miller brought with him a list of the techniques that Rumsfeld had authorized on April 16, 2003, for Guantanamo. Miller also explicitly recommended the use of dogs—although he claims for prisoner control only and not for interrogations.

On September 14, 2003, within days of Miller's departure, Lieutenant General Ricardo Sanchez, the chief of military operations in Iraq, authorized the use of a number of the Rumsfeld techniques about which he had been informed by Major General Miller. They included the aggressive use of dogs. Central Command of U.S. troops in Qatar, when it learned of Sanchez's order, countermanded it. But the damage was done. Gitmo had come to Baghdad.

Military personnel also traveled to Iraq from Afghanistan. In July and August 2003, a military intelligence unit from the Bagram Air Force Base in Afghanistan arrived at Abu Ghraib for interrogation duty. The harsh techniques that they brought with them resembled those in Guantanamo, including the removal of clothing, stress positions, and dogs.

A third source contributed to the problem at Abu Ghraib. CIA interrogators also worked there, and they did not follow the Army *Field Manual* rules, which provide clear and specific guidance on proper prisoner interrogation. The perception of a no-holds-barred ethos by the CIA "encouraged soldiers to deviate from prescribed techniques," according to a later report on abuse by Lieutenant General Anthony R. Jones.

The president's obligations were clear. Having personally created Geneva Convention exemptions, President Bush knew or should have known that there was a danger of migration of nonpermissible interrogation methods to Iraq. Once the Iraq War began, the president should have taken extra measures to underscore that the Geneva Conventions, the War Crimes Act, and the military manual on interrogations were all to be followed scrupulously.

President Bush had been warned by his own counsel, Gonzales, on January 25, 2002, that abandoning Geneva Conventions could "undermine military culture." The warning, which Bush ignored, turned out to be correct. Without a firm anchor in the rules of the Army *Field Manual* and its rejection of violence, humiliation, and cruelty, military personnel were left with a confusing mishmash, in addition to the knowledge that aggressive and cruel techniques had been approved by the president for use by U.S. personnel elsewhere under circumstances that looked quite similar.

The president was specially obligated to provide clear guidance to U.S. personnel and to "take care" that the laws were "faithfully executed," but he failed to do so.

THE TRAIL FROM THE PRESIDENT'S MEMO TO PRISONER ABUSE IN IRAQ

Several investigations confirmed an intolerable level of abuse of prisoners in Iraq. Painful and, in some cases, unbelievable, stories emerged. Nor was the abuse in Iraq limited to Abu Ghraib, but occurred at other U.S. detention facilities, as well.

One of the worst cases, described by the *Washington Post* in August 2005, took place at the Al-Qaim detention facility two hundred miles northwest of Baghdad. After going there voluntarily to look for his sons, Iraqi Major General Abed Hamed Mowhoush, age fifty-six, was held for sixteen days and interrogated brutally. He died in U.S. custody on November 26, 2003, two days after he was beaten so severely with fists, punches, a club, and a length of rubber hose that he had to be carried back to his cell. He died from asphyxia and chest compression in a session with U.S. Army interrogators who stuffed him into a sleeping bag, sat on him, and worked him over.

The ICRC, which is officially assigned as the monitor of the Geneva Conventions, issued a twenty-four-page report in February 2004 that found "systemic" mistreatment of Iraqi prisoners, especially "high value" detainees, in several facilities. The ICRC directly witnessed and documented "physical and psychological coercion" as "standard operating procedures by military intelligence" that included "holding people naked in a completely dark and empty cell for a prolonged period to use inhumane and degrading treatment; . . . Beatings with hard objects (including pistols and rifles), Slapping, punching, kicking with knees or feet on various parts of the body (legs, sides lower back, groin); Pressing the face into the ground with boots; . . . Being paraded naked outside cells . . . sometimes hooded, or with women's underwear over the head." The ICRC found psychological distress including "incoherent speech, acute anxiety reactions, abnormal behavior and suicidal tendencies." Investigators wrote, "These symptoms appeared to have been caused by the methods and durations of interrogations."

"The Schlesinger Report" confirmed in August 2004 that the abuses were "widespread" and "serious both in number and in effect." It was not the "failure of a few individuals" or the "failure of a few leaders to enforce proper discipline." There is both "institutional and personal responsibility at higher levels," the panel said. The stage for abuse was set, the panel said, by "fundamental failures throughout all levels of command, from the soldiers on the ground to [U.S.] Central Command and to the Pentagon."

In addition to physical and mental abuse of detainees, there were other violations of the Geneva Conventions in Iraq. Certain prisoners were hidden from the ICRC. Rumsfeld admitted during a press conference in June 2004 that, at the request of CIA Director George Tenet, he personally ordered the hiding of a detainee named Hiwa Abdul Rahman Rashul from the Red Cross inspection team. He admitted that other instances of "ghosting" had occurred.

The CIA also improperly transported Iraq prisoners out of Iraq for interrogations. These transfers kept the prisoners hidden from the ICRC, and may have facilitated brutal interrogations.

THE PRESIDENT'S FAILURE
TO BRING TOP OFFICIALS TO JUSTICE

The obligation to search out and prosecute all those potentially responsible for torture and mistreatment is written into the Geneva Conventions. Under them, the United States is explicitly required to bring before the courts those alleged to have committed "grave breaches." The government is required to "search for persons alleged to have committed . . . grave breaches," or those who have ordered them to be committed.

The president's obligation to faithfully execute the laws, including the War Crimes Act and Anti-Torture Act, similarly requires a full investigation into wrongdoing.

Under principles of "command responsibility," the president also has a duty to conduct a full investigation.

Despite these obligations, the president has failed to demand a full and complete investigation of the reports of torture or cruel, inhuman, and degrading treatment. No investigation reviewed the conduct of the highest civilian and military leaders; it appears that no investigation has been undertaken at all of CIA employees of any rank.

After the Abu Ghraib incidents were revealed, Rumsfeld told the Senate Armed Services Committee on May 7, 2004, "These events occurred on my watch as secretary of defense. I am accountable for them. I take full responsibility, I feel terrible about what happened to these detainees. They are human beings, they were in U.S. custody, our country had an obligation to treat them right. We didn't. That was wrong."

Although Rumsfeld, in essence, admitted to acts that violated the Geneva Conventions, the president said he rejected Rumsfeld's offers to resign. Bush has since commended him at least twice for doing "a fine job," and left him in charge of investigations of abusive treatment.

Rumsfeld made much ado of setting in motion a number of investigations into the treatment of detainees, creating the appearance of a comprehensive inquiry. But each inquiry was limited in scope; this flurry of activity was nothing more than a smokescreen that effectively shielded those at the highest levels from accountability.

Major General Taguba was assigned to investigate only the military police at Abu Ghraib. Major General George Fay was to study only military intelligence at Abu Ghraib, while Lieutenant General Anthony R. Jones investigated the 205th Military Intelligence Brigade and chain of command, so long as he did not go above the lieutenant general rank. The army inspector general was tasked with an analysis of army operations, but was not to undertake "investigation of any specific incidents or units."

Only one investigation—led by former Defense Secretary Schlesinger—was even permitted to question the top civilian and military brass. This panel was handpicked by Rumsfeld and asked merely to review the other investigations. It could not review CIA activities, and its instructions suggested that

there was no need to look at "issues of personal accountability" because those "will be resolved through established
military justice and administrative procedures."

None of these "procedures" was ever put into effect for
the highest military or civilian levels. The CIA has conducted
little in the way of public examination, as even a CIA
spokesperson acknowledged. So no one looked or is looking.
As a result, most of those disciplined are on the bottom
rungs. One lieutenant colonel faces criminal charges; one
brigadier general was given a reprimand and suspended. The
highest rank of any person convicted is a single captain, and
he received forty-five days in jail for kicking detainees and
staging a mock execution. It is almost as though the Watergate investigation stopped at the burglars—which is what the
Nixon White House tried to accomplish but was prevented
from doing.

Of 800 investigations, the Department of Defense said that
it took action against 251 service personnel. Of those, 232 suffered minor or no consequences, and 19 received sentences of
one year or more, according to U.S. officials reporting to the
UN Committee against Torture. The UN Committee, in
response, expressed concern about "limited investigation and
lack of prosecution," as well as "lenient sentences, including of
an administrative nature or less than one year's imprisonment."

President Bush is ultimately responsible. By permitting
Secretary Rumsfeld to structure and shape the investigations,
the president failed in his responsibilities in two key ways.
First, the secretary has no authority to enforce the War

Crimes Act or the Anti-Torture Act, which are the laws that would cover the civilian chain of command and the CIA. Second, Rumsfeld personally approved at least some of the military's harsh interrogation techniques, as well as "ghosting" of a detainee, and is himself an obvious subject of any serious investigation into the torture scandal. Giving control of an investigation to a person who should be reviewed by it for misconduct clearly makes a sham of the process.

If the president were serious about tracking down all who bear responsibility for the torture, he would establish an independent commission. For credibility's sake, Rumsfeld should not select the members and they should not be beneath him in the chain of command. (The president should also create a commission that is independent of Attorney General Gonzales and others who had a role in promulgating the rules that led to torture.) Alternatively, the president could seek the appointment of a special prosecutor who can determine whether federal criminal laws were violated.

An independent panel or special prosecutor might ask:

- What is the exact knowledge and role of Secretary Rumsfeld and top civilian and military brass with respect to the torture or cruel, inhuman, or degrading treatment of detainees, as well as the exact knowledge of the president? Have they met their obligations under the Geneva Conventions, War Crimes Act, the Convention against Torture, and the federal Anti-Torture Act?

- To what extent did CIA employees engage in torture or cruel and degrading treatment of U.S. detainees, and did such treatment violate the War Crimes or Anti-Torture Act? What was the exact role and state of knowledge of the CIA Director Tenet and President Bush? Did they violate the laws?

- What happened to "ghost detainees" in Iraq who were concealed from the International Committee of the Red Cross? Was the concealment ordered, requested, or authorized by Secretary Rumsfeld, CIA Director Tenet, or others to facilitate or cover up torture or cruel and degrading treatment? Did they violate the War Crimes or Anti-Torture Act? What role did the president play in authorizing or condoning the concealment and failure to investigate or punish it? Did he violate any U.S. criminal laws?

- What was the extent of the president's information about the cruel, inhuman, or degrading treatment of detainees prior to public awareness of the Abu Ghraib scandal? Was he informed of ICRC complaints about treatment of detainees in Iraq or elsewhere? What action did he take in response to any information? Is he liable under the War Crimes or the Anti-Torture Act?

- Did any torture or mistreatment of detainees occur in Afghanistan prior to the president's February 7, 2002, memo that stated the Geneva Conventions would have limited applicability? Since the Geneva Conventions applied until that date, are there violations of them, the

War Crimes Act, or antitorture laws, and who bears responsibility for those acts?

The UN Commission against Torture said in May 2006 that the United States "should promptly, thoroughly, and impartially investigate any responsibility of senior military and civilian officials authorizing, acquiescing or consenting, in any way, to acts of torture committed by their subordinates."

The president has not only failed to "search out" all responsible wrongdoers, but he has rewarded many of the planners and promulgators of torture techniques, a sign that that he condones their actions. The president has refused to fire, discipline, or reprimand Rumsfeld. The president bestowed the Medal of Freedom on former CIA Director Tenet, even though detainees died while in CIA custody and were hidden from international monitors at his request. After promulgating a plan to avoid the War Crimes Act, Gonzales was appointed attorney general. Lieutenant General Sanchez, who oversaw the detention facilities in Iraq, was promoted to the head of the Army's V Corps in Europe. Others were treated similarly.

The president is charged with upholding the laws, including those against war crimes. As commander in chief, he holds unique responsibility for the military. By failing to take the necessary actions to assure full accountability, he condones the use of torture and cruel, inhumane, and degrading treatment, and allows an unacceptable cover-up. These acts are impeachable offenses.

THE PRESIDENT'S COMMAND RESPONSIBILITY REQUIRES HIM TO TAKE ACTION AGAINST TORTURE

The concept of "command responsibility" arises under international law and U.S. principles in connection with war crimes. Under command responsibility principles established after World War II at the Nuremberg Trials of major Nazi war criminals, commanders are held criminally responsible for atrocities committed by their subordinates during war or occupation. The U.S. Supreme Court established the principle of command responsibility in the case of Japanese General Tomoyuki Yamashita, the head of the Japanese armies in the Philippines. Even though he had lost control of some of his troops when the United States invaded the Philippines, the United States tried the general for war crimes, including the brutal treatment of POWs by his troops and atrocities on more than 25,000 civilians. The Supreme Court upheld the verdict against Yamashita and he was executed.

Guilt under command responsibility can be established even if the commander did not order the atrocities, but knew or was put on notice of an atrocity, and failed to stop it or punish it.

The same standard has been applied to civilian leaders. For example, Slobodan Milosevic, the former president of Serbia, was put on trial at the Hague for numerous atrocities, including genocide, carried out under his leadership. Milosevic died in prison before the proceedings were finished.

Essentially, command responsibility is another way of formulating the mandate in the U.S. Constitution that the president must "take care" to faithfully execute the laws. Just as commanders cannot close their eyes to atrocities and must curb them, so the president of the United States cannot, when he is put on notice of the commission of war crimes by U.S. personnel, act with indifference. Command responsibility, like the "take care" clause, imposes an affirmative obligation to stop the atrocities and require punishment for them.

As noted previously, President Bush was put on notice as early as January 25, 2002, by a memo from Gonzales of possible atrocities—already committed or about to be committed. Command responsibility required the president to take all reasonable steps to stop or prevent the atrocities. He did not do that; instead, he facilitated the commission of atrocities by protecting perpetrators from criminal liability under the U.S. War Crimes Act. In addition, he deliberately imposed no constraints on CIA officers in their treatment of prisoners.

When the Abu Ghraib scandal broke out, the concept of command responsibility, just like the "take care" clause, required the president to take all reasonable steps to ascertain guilt and impose punishment. But he failed to do so and allowed Secretary Rumsfeld, who admitted responsibility for abuse that occurred on his "watch," to take charge of the investigations. The predictable result, as noted, is that the investigations failed to scrutinize those at the top of the ladder—senior officials and executives in the Pentagon, CIA, and White

House. Similarly, President Bush's praise for Rumsfeld, despite the torture scandal, violates command responsibility by sending troops a message that brutal mistreatment will be tolerated.

Under either formulation—command responsibility or the "take care" clause—the president cannot condone atrocities but must prevent or punish them, although the consequences are different. Command responsibility would impose punishment on the president; impeachment simply removes him from office.

THE PRESIDENT'S FAILURE TO PREVENT TORTURE IS AN ONGOING PROBLEM

The president has indicated that he will continue to disregard the law and to permit abusive conditions to continue. When Republican Senator John McCain, a former prisoner of war in Vietnam and a political conservative, rallied the Congress in 2005 to pass an amendment to the 2006 National Defense Authorization Bill to prohibit the "cruel, inhuman and degrading" treatment of detainees in U.S. military custody, the president lobbied against it.

So did the vice president, who, after 9/11, took to the airwaves to declare on *Meet the Press*: "We have to work, through, sort of the dark side, if you will." Cheney played a key role in opposing the McCain amendment and urged that the CIA be exempted.

The "dark side" lost in the Congressional battle when the Senate passed the new antitorture legislation 90 to 9 and the

House joined in to provide a veto-proof margin. But when the president signed it, he issued a frightening "signing statement," declaring that he was not bound by the law. "The Executive branch shall construe the act . . . in a manner consistent with . . . protecting the American people from further terrorist attacks," he declared. The president said, in essence, that he could ignore a law passed specifically to restrain him from allowing torture.

Senator Lindsay Graham, a conservative member of the Armed Services Committee, said, "I do not believe that any political figure in the country has the ability to set aside any . . . law of armed conflict that we have adopted or treaties that we have ratified. If we go down that road, it will cause great problems for our troops in future conflicts."

In May 2006, despite the clear language of the new law prohibiting torture against all detainees, Rumsfeld told the Senate Appropriations Committee that he wanted to see approval of two different interrogation techniques in the Army *Field Manual*—one for a "prisoner of war under the Geneva Conventions" and another for "an unlawful combatant." But confusing rules were a core problem that helped torture breed at Abu Ghraib. The secretary's position violates the McCain amendment.

The United States has been criticized severely for its policies against detainees, by allies and enemies alike. British Attorney General Peter Goldsmith called for the detention facility at Guantanamo to be closed as "an unacceptable symbol of injustice." The UN Committee against

Torture also urged the United States to end secret detentions and interrogation techniques that constitute torture or cruel, inhuman, or degrading treatment, including sexual humiliation, "water boarding," and the use of dogs to induce fear.

Some criticisms of the policies came from within the government, as well. According to documents released under the Freedom of Information Act, FBI officers at Guantanamo refused to use or participate in the aggressive interrogations that they saw and heard from military personnel. The Abu Ghraib torture was reported by one soldier, Specialist Joseph M. Darby, who simply believed it was wrong.

And Navy General Counsel Alberto J. Mora, since retired, fought a courageous three-year battle inside the Pentagon to stop policies that permitted cruelty and torture. "If cruelty is no longer declared unlawful, but instead is applied as a matter of policy, it alters the fundamental relationship of man to government. . . . If you make this exception, the whole Constitution crumbles," Mora told *New Yorker* writer Jane Mayer. "The debate here isn't only how to protect the country. It's how to protect our values."

CONCLUSION: WHY IMPEACHMENT IS NECESSARY FOR PRESIDENTIAL ACTS IN PERMITTING OR CONDONING TORTURE OR MISTREATMENT OF DETAINEES

"We do not torture," President Bush has said on more than one occasion. Against the mass of the evidence of abuse, deaths, and degrading tactics used at Abu Ghraib and other U.S. military detention facilities, the phrase is surreal. It is not unlike President Nixon's infamous comment—"I am not a crook"—when evidence all around him spoke differently.

The United States has adopted laws and ratified treaties prohibiting the mistreatment or torture of prisoners in U.S. hands. As president, Bush is responsible for implementing and enforcing them. But he did not. The torture that we saw was set in motion when President Bush gave the CIA carte blanche in the treatment of detainees and when he removed application of the well-established and carefully developed protections of the Geneva Conventions for CIA and military interrogators.

The president did not take actions consistent with the requirements of the Constitution—or even with his public statements on torture. To the contrary, he refused to discipline or fire the higher-ups who were responsible. He failed to require a full investigation and punishment for all involved. In his recent action, the president added a signing statement to the new McCain antitorture legislation, declaring that he has the right to violate that law at will.

Impeachment is the only way to prevent the president from continuing a policy that condones torture and mistreatment. And it is the only way to put an end to his refusal to carry out his obligation to "take care" that the laws are faithfully executed.

CHAPTER SIX

Impeachment for Reckless Indifference to Human Life: Katrina and Iraq

OVERVIEW

In 2003, the father of a Pennsylvania reservist began receiving frantic calls from his son in Iraq. The U.S. military had deployed the son to a battle zone without providing him with adequate body armor. Desperate with worry, the father wrote a personal check for the equipment and sent it.

Another parent is not so lucky. In 2004, she tried to make sense of events as she stood beside the coffin of her son, a sergeant killed in a building explosion in Iraq more than a year after May 1, 2003, the date on which the president declared that "major combat operations had ended." Her son died, not in the six weeks of "major combat," but during a postinvasion occupation so misguided and badly planned that thousands lost their lives or suffered bodily harm.

In the 2005 aftermath of Hurricane Katrina, an elderly New Orleans woman sought to explain how she and her husband had scrambled for safety onto their rooftop. But as the waters unleashed by the city's broken levees rose, she watched helplessly as he was overcome by the rapidly rising waters and washed away.

These newspapers and magazine stories about people coping with harsh circumstances, while disparate, are linked by the colossal failures of President George W. Bush. In each situation, people have suffered endangerment and harm, even death, because of conduct by the president that shows a wanton, gross, and reckless indifference to human life.

President Bush is required under the Constitution to "take care" that the laws are faithfully executed. He has failed to do so, and his failures in at least three instances are grounds for impeachment:

- He failed as president and "commander in chief" of disaster relief to mobilize federal resources to deal with the devastation of Hurricane Katrina, causing unnecessary human suffering and loss of life.
- He failed to "take care" as commander in chief and president to ensure that U.S. soldiers in Iraq were protected with body armor and shielded vehicles, exposing troops to unnecessary risks of death or bodily harm.

- He failed as commander in chief and as president to plan for the occupation of Iraq, allowing an insurgency to take firm root. The result has cost the lives of more than two thousand five hundred Americans and the wounding of thousands of others, as well as the loss of countless Iraqi lives.

In each of these instances, the president was personally responsible for action as commander in chief or as president. In each instance, thousands of lives were at stake. In each instance, he was derelict in his duty, displaying reckless indifference to human life, failing to carry out his oath of office and his responsibilities as president. These are high crimes or misdemeanors for which he should be impeached.

THE CONSTITUTION AND GROSS INDIFFERENCE TO HUMAN LIFE

Major failures on the part of the president to fulfill his oath of office in situations of extraordinary emergency and potential harm to Americans extend beyond mere simple negligence and are grounds for impeachment. President Bush is guilty of such failures.

The framers of our Constitution understood when they drafted the impeachment clause that a president should not be removed for "maladministration." When presidential neglect involves carelessness or mistakes, impeachment is not available. Instead, impeachment is meant to be a lifeboat for the country when the captain steers the ship of state into a pile of rocks.

When the president's conduct or negligence crosses the line into wanton, gross, and reckless indifference to human life on a scale of great magnitude, he is no longer in a no-impeachment zone. He violates his duty to "take care" that the laws are faithfully executed. This is a high crime and misdemeanor.

In three critical instances, the president crossed this line— in his failure to mobilize U.S. resources for disaster relief, to provide armor, and to plan for an insurgency. President Bush's actions in these situations show a wanton, gross, and reckless indifference to human life and violate his duty to "take care."

IMPEACHABLE OFFENSES IN FAILING TO ATTEND TO THE IMMINENT CATASTROPHE FACING NEW ORLEANS FROM HURRICANE KATRINA

People on the Gulf Coast of the United States lived through unimaginable conditions in the days and weeks and months after Hurricane Katrina hit on August 29, 2005. The damage resulted from outrageous failures in the nation's emergency response systems during one of the nation's worst natural disasters. The inadequate evacuation, along with levee collapse, flooding, property destruction, abandonment, and deaths in the aftermath of Hurricane Katrina were worsened by the recklessness indifference of President Bush, who, as the "commander-in-chief of disaster response," was responsible for overseeing federal emergency response.

Hurricane Katrina survivors slogged through floodwaters that overcame weakened levees, while the rest of the nation watched aghast. Meanwhile, the president vacationed and attended a fund-raiser. Other Katrina victims died and suffered because of a slack and bumbling emergency response. Many more faced harm in emergency shelters that lacked necessary supplies.

The awful scenes of terrified citizens trapped in extreme heat on roofs, in water, in an overflowing stadium, without food, water, medicine, or emergency provisions extended beyond the Katrina disaster. The week opened a window into the utter inadequacy of President Bush in preparing for and responding to disaster conditions, whether from causes of nature or terrorism.

Americans reacted generously, pouring out donations and offering services to Katrina victims. President Bush was AWOL . . . absent without leave. He failed to "take care" to see that the laws were faithfully executed. Even though the laws gave him the unique power to mobilize resources and save lives, he did not respond to emergency needs.

Early and strong presidential involvement is key to mitigating the effects of a disaster and saving human life—so much so that the president is considered the "commander-in-chief of disaster relief," in the words of the House of Representatives committee investigating emergency response to Katrina. The president, and only the president, can issue emergency orders to mobilize the military and any federal resources needed to aid and assist in a disaster.

When catastrophe strikes, the capacity of states and localities to assist is quickly overwhelmed. In such cases, federal law provides for a much stronger, essentially preemptive role for the federal government. President Bush failed to discharge his personal responsibility under federal law to mobilize resources to respond to the disaster.

Additionally, he appointed disaster officials who were hapless in the face of a major natural disaster.

The primary impact of the hurricane's aftermath landed on those least able to fend for themselves: the poor, the sick, and the elderly, many of whom were African American. Hundreds of thousands of people on the Gulf Coast suffered because of the president's failure to act. More than 1,300 people died and more than 2,000 are missing.

The president's inertia and indifference, despite clear warnings and direct firsthand reports to him of a pending disaster, is a high crime and misdemeanor for which he should be impeached.

BACKGROUND OF PRESIDENTIAL ROLE IN DISASTER RELIEF

The Stafford Act of the federal government creates the legal framework for responding to disasters (42 U.S.C. Section 5122). According to *Failure of Initiative*, a February 2006 report of the House Select Bipartisan Committee to Investigate the Preparations for and the Response to Hurricane Katrina, "The Stafford Act places the federal government's disaster response authorities with the President. Similar to military matters, the President is the *commander in chief of federal disaster response*" (emphasis added).

Disaster professionals knew that New Orleans was vulnerable

to a strong hurricane, category 3 or larger. For years, the possible breach of the levees has rated as one of the three likeliest, and deadliest, potential disasters in the United States. Many sections of the city, including some of the poorest neighborhoods, lie below sea level by as much as ten feet. Only an aging levee system held back the waters that surrounded the city, including the large Lake Pontchartrain on the northern edge. If the levees crumbled or were topped, floods would rage through the streets and into yards, homes, businesses, and hospitals. Research conducted in 2004 indicated that sixty thousand lives could be lost if the levees were breached.

Despite these predictions, President Bush repeatedly cut funds for the Army Corps of Engineers to work on the levees. Pleas for funding for a better pumping system to prevent and mitigate flooding went unanswered.

The president's failure to understand or act upon his role as the commander in chief of disaster relief is particularly glaring in light of 9/11. That attack made it absolutely clear that the nation needed to plan for effective and rapid emergency response to disasters of great scope and magnitude. The creation of the Department of Homeland Security and the development of a National Response Program under the Stafford Act were designed to establish a proactive and coordinated federal response when states and localities are overwhelmed.

The president also failed by appointing unqualified people to the top positions at the federal agencies specifically responsible for disaster relief. Michael Brown, appointed by the president as the head of Federal Emergency Management

Agency (FEMA), had no background whatsoever in disaster relief. He was, in the words of *New York Times* columnist Paul Krugman, a "crony," a college friend of Bush's campaign manager. His previous experience was as head of the International Arabian Horses Association. Brown's top aides were also chosen because of their political connections and did not have expertise in disaster relief.

Brown's boss, Michael Chertoff, secretary of the Department of Homeland Security that oversees FEMA, was also appointed by the president and lacked experience in disaster relief. Chertoff, an experienced federal prosecutor and former federal judge, is clearly qualified to handle issues of terrorism. But disaster relief is a significant aspect of the job. The House Select Committee noted that Chertoff is "not a hurricane expert, nor does he have much experience with disasters."

In his appointments, the president failed to appreciate the federal government's responsibility under the law to save human lives and mitigate suffering in a disaster.

President Bush acknowledged that after 9/11 "Americans have a right to expect a more effective response in a time of emergency."

The president had almost four full years from the events of 9/11 to put a proper mechanism in place staffed by knowledgeable and expert professionals to deal with disasters. But he did not do this. The president is directly responsible for federal disaster coordination. His failure is inexcusable and laid the groundwork for the unnecessary consequences of Katrina.

EVIDENCE OF FAILURES IN KATRINA RESCUE OPERATIONS

Warnings about the threat posed by Hurricane Katrina came days in advance. More than fifty-six hours before landfall, meteorologists predicted the New Orleans could be in the direct path of a category 5 hurricane. By the time it made landfall, Katrina was deemed a category 4 hurricane (ultimately designated level 3 on the Saffir-Simpson scale), but a ferocious one. Katrina had 125 mile-an-hour winds and huge storm surges that washed the land with walls of water ranging between 18 and 27 feet high. By contrast the levees in New Orleans reached only 17 feet.

Despite ample warnings about the hurricane and the first-ever evacuation order issued by a mayor of New Orleans, no proper federal evacuation plan was in place. A disaster exercise in 2004 indicated that widespread flooding would leave 200,000 to 300,000 in need of evacuation if a major hurricane hit New Orleans. Federal officials "knew that state and local authorities would need evacuation help," according the May 2006 report of the Senate Committee on Homeland Security and Governmental Affairs, *Hurricane Katrina: A Nation Still Unprepared.*

The nation was aware that Katrina was headed for New Orleans and the surrounding areas. President Bush, even if he did not read the newspapers, was specifically informed on Saturday, August 27, 2005. On that day, Louisiana Governor Kathleen Blanco requested that President Bush designate the state as a disaster area. President Bush, alerted to the severity of the situation, complied.

On the afternoon of Sunday, August 28, a Louisiana news-paper warned that the levees might not hold. Approximately 30,000 people followed orders to evacuate to the Superdome; there were supplies for only one and one-half days. Louisiana sought 700 buses from the federal government; only 100 arrived.

Dr. Max Mayfield, director of the National Hurricane Center, updated Brown and Chertoff about the dangers on August 28th, before the hurricane hit. "We were briefing them way before landfall," said Mayfield. "It's not like this was a sur-prise." In advisories that day, Mayfield said that the levees could be topped. He warned about the fierce storm surge.

On August 28 at about 11 A.M., the president was person-ally briefed at his ranch in Texas about the dire situation by a video conference with top officials, including Maxfield. A transcript and videotape of that briefing show that President Bush was informed in person of critical facts. The hurricane had "maximum intensity," said Dr. Mayfield. The possible topping of the levees, said Mayfield, is "obviously a very, very grave concern." The situation presented a great potential for the loss of lives, he said.

A second essential fact was communicated to the president in the briefing. Brown said that New Orleans faced a "catas-trophe." Despite the gravity of the warnings, President Bush seemed curiously detached and did not ask a single question.

The House Select Committee Report noted that "cata-strophic disasters require early presidential involvement to reduce the loss of life, human suffering, and extensive prop-erty damage." But that early presidential involvement did not take place. The president, the House committee noted, did not "fully engage."

During the briefing, the president was asked to comment. He said, "I want to assure the folks at the state level that, ahh, we are fully prepared to not only help you during the storm but we will move in whatever resources and assets we have at our disposal after the storm to help you deal with the loss of property and we, ahh, pray for no loss of life, of course." He continued, "The FEMA folks have done great work in the past. . . . In the meantime, I know the nation will be praying for the good folks in the affected areas, and we just hope for the very best."

The president, with vast resources at his disposal, did not bother to ask what would happen if the levees were breached; whether there was a plan for evacuation and how good it was; whether there was an adequate framework for rescue; whether he should marshal assistance from the military; whether there would be food, water, and other supplies for those in need—or whether there was anything else in his powers as president and commander in chief of disaster relief that he could do to provide emergency resources. He didn't ask how the matter was being coordinated among federal agencies or by his subordinates. President Bush gave no orders or directions for any action. Although he did say that he expected people to keep "long hours," he apparently didn't have any idea how they should fill them. He did not seek advice or solicit further details about what he needed to do to implement the most effective response under the

National Response Plan, the document that guides federal response to disasters.

If the president had faithfully implemented the law or acted on his responsibility as the "commander in chief of disaster relief," he would have asked many questions and demanded action. If he had asked even one question, he would have learned that federal preparations were utterly inadequate and needed to be massively upgraded. He would have realized that the federal government's incompetence, incoherence, and ineffectiveness would contribute to the huge loss of life and suffering. But he never asked. He only offered empty words.

Other than convening the briefing, Brown didn't know what else to do either. He "lacked the leadership skills that were needed," said the Senate committee investigating the rescue efforts. "Brown did not direct the adequate pre-positioning of critical personnel and equipment." Only one medical team was prepositioned to provide immediate medical care. Chertoff, the Senate committee noted, did not activate a critical rule, the Catastrophic Incident Annex to the National Response Program, which would have signaled all federal agencies to get moving.

On the morning of Monday, August 29, Katrina made landfall. The Bush administration was notified of a levee breach and e-mails circulated throughout the White House. The mayor reported that a pumping station was not operating and flooding could be expected.

Later on Monday August 29, a section of the 17th Street Canal collapsed. Governor Blanco requested urgent assistance from the president. "Mr. President, we need your help. We need everything you've got," she said. The president did not respond.

President Bush, as it happens, was occupied with other matters. He visited senior centers to promote his Medicare prescription drug program and stopped for a special photo-op to celebrate Senator John McCain's birthday. He spoke with Secretary of Homeland Security Chertoff about immigration. He took no action to aid the people facing catastrophe.

On Tuesday, August 30, the mayor of New Orleans opened the convention center as an alternative shelter, and nineteen thousand people converged on it. Food and water were not available. The Louisiana deputy director of emergency preparedness begged the federal government to ratchet up "the sense of urgency."

President Bush made a speech that day at a naval base and played guitar with country singer Mark Willis, then returned to his ranch to continue his vacation for several more days. He did nothing to marshal a response from Texas, and said he would "begin work" after he flew back to Washington on Thursday. During this critical time period, people were frantic for help in New Orleans.

A bipartisan Senate committee later criticized the president for this inexplicable delay in coordinating assistance for one of the nation's worst natural disasters. "The president is, after all, the commander in chief—not only in terms of international crises, but in terms of catastrophes here at home," said Senator Joe Lieberman.

On the morning of Wednesday, August 31, Brown was warned that people were dying at the Superdome, where tens of thousands were trapped and already atrocious conditions were deteriorating. President Bush flew back to Washington, flying over the areas devastated by Hurricane Katrina on Air Force One. A photographer took a picture of him looking out the window.

On Thursday, September 1, President Bush appeared on *Good Morning America*. Defending his failure to respond to the hurricane, he said, "I don't think that anybody anticipated a breach of the levees." But President Bush had been personally informed of the possible overrunning of the levees four days earlier, although the falsity of his TV statement did not become apparent until March 2006 when a videotape was released and it showed that he was fully briefed in advance.

On Thursday evening, for the first time, FEMA asked the Department of Defense to take over the logistics. The Department of Defense had been on hold until then.

On Friday, September 2, 2005, President Bush traveled on an inspection mission to the Gulf States and New Orleans. Louisiana Senator Mary Landrieu accused him of staging a photo-op. Press reports state that on the flight there, one of the president's aides gave Bush a DVD of the week's newscasts so that the horrific reality of what was happening in New Orleans and the surrounding areas would sink in.

No sense of urgency existed in the Bush administration. Vice President Cheney was on vacation and stayed there. Secretary of State Rice was shoe-shopping in New York. Defense

Secretary Rumsfeld took in a baseball game in San Diego on August 29.

Not until Saturday, September 3, 2005, did the president send federal ground troops to aid with evacuation of the city, as the National Response Plan permits the president to do in cases of disaster, according to the Senate committee's report, *A Nation Still Unprepared*.

"It's unclear why President Bush waited until Saturday to deploy federal troops," said the Senate committee. "The fecklessness of the government response became a story unto itself."

WHY IMPEACHMENT IS NECESSARY FOR BUSH'S FAILURE TO RESPOND TO DISASTER

The federal response to the hurricane was woefully inadequate. The blame lies directly with President Bush.

While presidential detachment may not have fatal consequences in many situations, it did with respect to Hurricane Katrina, particularly because of the structure of the federal laws on disaster response. The federal government is responsible for supplementing states and localities when called upon to do so.

As "commander in chief of federal disaster response," President Bush failed to direct a response to the catastrophe of Katrina, something that required "early presidential involvement to direct federal agencies in a massive coordinated response," according to the House Select Committee.

The president failed to ensure that the federal government and its agencies were mobilized beforehand. Once the catastrophe hit, the president failed to coordinate and send the resources needed to save people's lives and provide rescue efforts. Finally, the president has failed to help the people of the region get back on their feet, and many struggle with dislocation, housing, finances, and family reunion.

Despite urgent needs in New Orleans, the president failed to activate the Department of Defense, even though it was in his sole power to do so. According the analysis of the House Committee, under the Stafford Act "only the President appears able to promptly engage active duty military forces and achieve a unity of effort among all the federal agencies responding to a catastrophic disaster."

In failing to fulfill his responsibilities under the Stafford Act in the face of a looming disaster of staggering proportions, President Bush failed to "take care" that the laws were "faithfully executed," a high crime and misdemeanor. The result was the unnecessary loss of life, human suffering, property damage, and destruction to one of America's great cities.

To cover up his recklessness, President Bush has refused to release all the e-mail and other documents showing what he knew and when he knew it. The implication is that those documents will reinforce the conclusion of the House Select Committee that he was not "fully engage[d]" in responding to the unfolding catastrophe.

The president tried to cover up his failure to respond with false statements to the American people. In addition to denying his advance knowledge at the time, in an ABC interview on February 28, 2006, President Bush said, "Listen, here's the problem that happened in Katrina. There was no situational awareness, and that means that we weren't getting good, solid information from people who were on the ground, and we need to do a better job."

This was also false, since people "on the ground"—from the director of the hurricane center to the Governor of Louisiana—provided the president directly and in person with "situational awareness" of the catastrophe. Every household in America with a television watched it unfold. More to the point, the difficulties arose from the president's lack of leadership, lack of preparation, and lack of mobilization of all necessary federal resources.

During the same ABC interview, President Bush was asked, "What moment do you think was the moment that you realized that the government was failing, especially the people of New Orleans?" The president responded, "When I saw TV reporters interviewing people who were screaming for help. It looked—the scenes looked chaotic and desperate. And I realized that our government was—could have done a better job of comforting people." He added, "It just—it was very unsettling for me to realize our fellow citizens were in near panic wondering where the help was."

Significantly, President Bush admitted that he understood there was a problem only after the hurricane hit—and not before. His recognition was not from briefings made to him or information circulating the White House. And, sad to say, he seemed to think that the major failing on the part of "our government" was in not "comforting people." Plainly, people might not have needed as much comforting if the federal government agencies under his control had reacted as they should have under disaster response laws.

The president also failed in his selection of disaster relief officials, as well as in his refusal to hold them accountable. Because he appointed individuals without the knowledge or ability to lead emergency services, neither Chertoff nor Brown insisted that the president assert his role as "commander in chief of federal disaster relief." The House Select Committee pointed out that Chertoff executed his responsibilities under the National Response Plan "late, ineffectively or not at all."

Despite the scathing criticism of Chertoff, the president has yet to hold him accountable. Chertoff remains at the helm of the Department of Homeland Security. President Bush said in February 2006 that "he is doing a fine job." (While Brown resigned from FEMA after a national outcry, the president previously and infamously told him, "Brownie, you're doing a heckuva job.")

Despite the enormous post 9/11 resources pured into disaster preparedness, President Bush was still not prepared to handle a great disaster when it struck in fact.

President Bush did not fulfill his responsibilities to ensure that the federal government delivered emergency resources in a grave situation. This wanton, gross, and reckless indifference to human life is a violation of presidential oath and of his duty to take care that the laws are faithfully executed. The president's further inability to grasp how he failed suggests that he is incapable of being the "commander in chief of disaster relief," as the law requires, putting all Americans at risk. For these reasons, President Bush deserves impeachment and removal from office.

IMPEACHABLE OFFENSES IN FAILING TO PLAN FOR THE SAFETY AND PROTECTION OF AMERICAN TROOPS

The president sent American troops into war in Iraq without an adequate number of bulletproof vests. They also did not have properly armored vehicles. Almost immediately after the invasion, soldiers implored relatives at home to buy them the lifesaving bulletproof vests.

At the start of the president's war in Iraq, nearly one out of three soldiers—40,000 of the 130,000 of the U.S. troops—lacked the basic protection of Kevlar Interceptor vests or the full protection of state-of-the-art ceramic inserts. Some soldiers were fighting with obsolete Vietnam-era equipment.

Six months after the start of the war, at a September 2003 hearing, concerned members of Congress demanded to know why soldiers were so unprotected. "I can't answer for the record why we started this war with protective vests that were in short supply," said General John Abizaid. Abizaid was the head of the U.S. Central Command and commander of all the military forces in Iraq.

The hardships posed by a lack of proper equipment were foreseen by people who cared about the safety and welfare of the troops. Senator Robert Byrd of West Virginia wrote to Secretary of Defense Rumsfeld on February 6, 2003, six weeks before the start of the war, to find out why National Guard units were being deployed to the Persian Gulf without desert camouflage uniforms. Senator Byrd called for "an immediate review to ensure that our troops are receiving the proper equipment for the environment in which they are being deployed."

Byrd received no reply to his call for a review. He later learned that units from his home state were deployed in Iraq without essential protective gear—ceramic inserts needed to maximize the effectiveness of their bulletproof vests. At a September 24, 2003, hearing Byrd asked Secretary of Defense Rumsfeld and General Richard P. Myers, chairman of the Joint Chiefs of Staff, to explain.

Rumsfeld prodded Myers to answer. "It's true that the ceramic breastplates, there were not enough of them on hand," said General Myers.

Secretary Rumsfeld, not satisfied, jumped in: "I believe they already have inserts. They're just not the insert that is being referred to . . . which is a ceramic insert. They have the vests, they have the inserts, but apparently the . . . the ceramic insert has been proved to be better. And as [a] result, it is being added."

Only after many more months did the Pentagon began to provide the proper protective vests. In 2005, some troops were still waiting for up-to-date body armor. The Marine Corps finally ordered ceramic side plates for 28,000 soldiers in September 2005, while the Army was still deciding on side plates in January 2006, according to an article by Michael Moss in the *New York Times* on January 6, 2006. Ultimately, in October 2005, Congress forced the military to reimburse troops for monies expended by their families for the vests, but reimbursement has moved slowly.

The military also lacked sufficient armored vehicles. Soldiers did their best to jerry-rig their Humvees with scraps of metal and sandbags to keep them from becoming death traps. They called it "hillbilly armor."

In one incident in October 2004, the 343rd Quartermaster Company, an Army Reserve unit from South Carolina, refused to obey orders to transport oil along a particularly attack-prone road because their convey was unarmored. The soldiers called it a "suicide mission." Eighteen members were arrested. After intense publicity over the incident, the commander resigned, and members of the company were disciplined but not court-martialed.

The absence of armor also prompted a highly publicized exchange in December 2004 between a soldier and Secretary of Defense Rumsfeld at a town hall meeting in Kuwait, where 2,300 troops were preparing to leave for Iraq. The army reservist wanted to know why the troops were forced to scrounge through garbage dumps to find material with which to reinforce their vehicles. "Why don't we have those resources readily available to us?" asked Army Specialist Thomas Wilson. Secretary Rumsfeld, caught off guard, responded, "As you know, you go to war with the army that you have, not the army you might want or wish to have at a later time."

Lack of armor leads to unnecessary deaths. The Pentagon knows this. The results of its own study, obtained by the *New York Times* and published in a January 6, 2006 article, found that the vast majority of marines who died of torso wounds— 80 percent—would have lived if they had been equipped with adequate protective plates. The lives of more than 300 army troops could have been saved with better protective body armor, according to the study.

Unlike Rumsfeld's glib response to soldiers entering a dangerous combat zone, the war was not in response to an attack or the imminent threat of attack. As described earlier, the president began planning for the war in 2002, if not before. The Pentagon and the president had more than a year to prepare before their March 19, 2003 invasion—plenty of time and opportunity to provide the troops with proper bulletproof vests and armored vehicles. But neither the Pentagon nor the president attended to the issue, even though it was a matter of life and death for U.S. troops. Propaganda was aplenty; proper preparations for safety and security of the troops were shortchanged.

Safety of the troops must be a central concern for a commander in chief and a secretary of defense. This was not the case. Those who act recklessly and fail to take due precautions must be held accountable for the resulting loss of lives.

The president also engaged in a cover-up. He told an audience in Kansas City on September 4, 2003, "My attitude is, any time we put one of our soldiers in harm's way, we're going to spend whatever is necessary to make sure they have the best training, the best support and the best possible equipment." It wasn't true. At that time, soldiers were being killed because of a lack of proper equipment.

George Washington University law professor Jonathan Turley investigated the decision to deploy troops without adequate armor. "The failure to supply all units with modern vests by the beginning of the war is a case of criminal negligence," wrote Turley in *The Hill* on October 7, 2003. Six months later, with soldiers still missing protective gear, Turley lamented to a newspaper reporter: "No one that I know of has been truly held accountable."

The president never rebuked Secretary Rumsfeld for his insensitive remarks to the troops, or for his failure to provide proper safety equipment for them. In April 2006, faced with calls for Rumsfeld to resign, President Bush said the defense secretary had done "a fine job" in conducting the war.

The president has personal accountability, as well. He decided to drive the country to war in March 2003, despite the lack of an imminent threat. The timetable for the invasion was not based on pressing military needs. British Prime Minister Tony Blair and President Bush met on January 31, 2003, and penciled in a start date for invading Iraq, even though no weapons of mass destruction had been found and UN inspectors were still at work searching for them. (See Chapter Three.)

The president, as commander in chief, bears ultimate responsibility. With no immediate threat and more than a year to prepare, the failure to protect troops with proper equipment is inexcusable. The president's failure to "take care" shows a wanton, gross, and reckless disregard for the lives of Americans he put in harm's way. This is an abuse of his power as commander in chief and a high crime and misdemeanor, for which he should be impeached.

IMPEACHABLE OFFENSES IN GOING TO WAR IN IRAQ WITHOUT AN ADEQUATE POSTINVASION PLAN

The rise of guerrilla warfare in Iraq was a foreseeable consequence of President Bush's decision to invade Iraq, but the president failed to plan for that eventuality, or for the occupation or the dangerous conditions that Americans would encounter. President Bush and members of his administration, claiming that Americans would be hailed as "liberators," failed to prepare adequately for what was known as "Phase IV"—the postinvasion period. As a consequence, resistance quickly mounted, making dangerous conditions for American troops, and killing and maiming thousands. The failure to plan shows recklessness and a gross indifference to human lives.

Acting Army Secretary Les Brownlee is one of many who acknowledged the failure: "Events since the end of major combat operations in Iraq have differed from our expectations and have combined to cause problems," Brownlee told Republican Senator John W. Warner in November 2003. Brownlee was discussing the issue of body armor, but that is only one of many disasters that the president's recklessness caused.

President Bush did not have an adequate postinvasion plan and did not have a backup strategy to deal with rapidly changing events. He acted with reckless indifference to the costs in lives and dollars.

The British recognized the president's failures as early as a year before the war, according to British documents leaked in 2005. David Manning, senior policy advisor to Prime Minister Blair, described his March 2002 dinner with National Security Advisor Condoleezza Rice. Iraq was the topic, and regime change was the main course. Manning wrote, "Bush has yet to find the answers to the big questions . . . what happens on the morning after?" The British assessment changed little. Blair's top advisors underscored this point in July 2002, writing that "little thought has been given to creating the political conditions for military action, or the aftermath and how to shape it." The postwar occupation of Iraq could be "protracted and costly," they warned. Also in July, after meetings in the United States, the chief of Britain's intelligence service weighed in with his concerns. "There was little discussion in Washington of the aftermath after military action."

Days before the March 19, 2003, invasion, Prime Minister Blair asked President Bush whether plans had been prepared for the occupation. President Bush told him that plans had been made. That was barely the truth, as the British—and Americans—soon discovered.

The U.S. "plans" were based on a fiction, perhaps even fantasy, picturing the Iraqis so shocked and awed that they would greet the American military as liberators, put down their arms, submerge long-standing sectarian rivalries, install the Pentagon friend and secular Shiite exile Ahmad Chalabi as leader of the country, keep their national institutions running smoothly, provide for the country's humanitarian and security needs, and celebrate their shotgun marriage with a new U.S. partner, which would take control of its oil fields.

The postwar operations were running on "blind faith," wrote an astonished British envoy John Sawers when he traveled to Iraq shortly after the invasion ended, according to documents published by Michael R. Gordon and General Bernard Trainor in their book, *Cobra II.* "An unbelievable mess," Sawers said. Planning was missing; so was reality.

"There was a failure to anticipate the extent of the backlash or mood of Iraqi society," added Britain's most senior military officer Major General Albert Whitley a few months later. "Is strategic failure a possibility? The answer has to be 'yes,'" he concluded.

These failures are directly attributable to President Bush's dereliction of duty and reckless and wanton indifference to the potential cost in human lives. Rather than utilize the plans of the State Department or Middle East experts who had studied Iraq for many years, Bush put Secretary of Defense Rumsfeld in charge of postwar planning. That was a mistake.

Rumsfeld held a simplistic and limited view of what the occupancy would entail. In a radio interview on November 14, 2002, he explained how the United States would handle the postwar period: "Number one, to find the weapons of mass destruction and destroy them. And number two, to see that the humanitarian assistance was provided. Number three, to see that the oil wells, to the extent they've been damaged, were back in working condition and providing the kind of revenue that's going to be necessary for the health and welfare of the people in that country. And then at some point, some sort of a provisional government of Iraqis would find its way in the world."

Unlike Secretary of State Colin Powell, who told the president and others about the consequences of invasion—that if "you break it, you own it"—meaning the invading nation is responsible for reconstruction and rebuilding—Rumsfeld decided that the military could smash the country and hand its fractured pieces back to Iraq to put together again. Rumsfeld said in another speech that he would not tolerate a "culture of dependency" by Iraqis after the invasion.

His narrow view, however, ignored what many knew: insurgents were likely to fight any outside occupying power. "The prevailing view within intelligence agencies . . . was that there would be resistance," noted Walter Pincus in a September 9, 2003 article in the *Washington Post*, "Spy Agencies Warned of Iraq Resistance."

When Army Chief of Staff General Eric K. Shinseki, assessing the likely rebellion in Iraq, told Congress in February 2003 that two or three times the troops estimated by Rumsfeld would be needed postinvasion to secure the country, the Bush administration promptly pushed him aside. Deputy Defense Secretary Paul Wolfowitz said Shinseki was "wildly off the mark." Shinseki based his predictions on the need for postwar security and troop strength to stabilize institutions and quell resistance. Shinseki was proven right.

The first signs of insurgency came during the march into in Iraq. Instead of Iraqis who showered praise and poetry, guerrilla fighters started shooting. Conservative columnist David Brooks wrote on March 16, 2006, "If Rumsfeld had made adjustments to the new circumstances then, much of the subsequent horror could have been averted." Rumsfeld, however, had paid no attention.

The needs for security and safety and basic services for Iraq did not figure in Rumsfeld's plans. He did not comprehend the need to create peace and order; provide food, clean water, fuel, lawful systems, and reconstruction; and the return of Iraq to normalcy. Under the international law principles in the 1907 Hague Regulations and the 1949 Fourth Geneva Convention, this is an unbending obligation of an occupying power. While refusing to be called "occupiers" at first, the United States finally accepted the designation of "occupying power" applied by the United Nations Security Council.

Rumsfeld's infamous comment on the lawlessness and vast looting of archaeological treasures, hospitals, and homes because of a lack of police security was, "Stuff happens."

All of this stuff happened predictably. Before the war, knowlegeable Iraqis warned about looting, but Rumsfeld ignored them. The Council on Foreign Relations advised that it would be essential to establish public security immediately—"critical to preventing lawlessness." A January 2003

National Intelligence Council report on "Principal Challenges in Post-Saddam Iraq" said Iraq was "a deeply divided society with a chance that domestic groups would engage in violent conflict" and that outside humanitarian assistance would be necessary, according to excerpts printed in the *New York Times* on March 13, 2006. The Army War College's Strategic Studies Institute published an in-depth report in February 2003 anticipating turmoil. The CIA warned of civil disorder. The State Department developed extensive expert studies for the occupation. But the president ignored all of this information.

Prior to the invasion, the United Institute for Peace, whose bipartisan members are appointed by the president, reported to the Defense Policy Board, also appointed by the president, that "the U.S. will quickly face the challenge of creating post-conflict security in Iraq. This task will be difficult, confusing and dangerous," according to documents published by Gordon and Trainor. The U.S. military, the institute said, will not be able to rely on local authorities and will require a separate police entity. This information was ignored.

The national intelligence officer for the region at the time, Paul R. Pillar, projected "a long, difficult and turbulent transition" with a divided society, violent conflict, and guerrilla warfare. He was ignored, as well.

The president's "plan A" was saddled with ineptitude and rife with flaws; no plan B existed. Backup planning is elementary. The idea of a swift victory so intrigued the president and top Pentagon officials that they had no alternative strategy. To this inadequate planning and nonexistent fall-back, the president signed his name.

Army Secretary Thomas White left the Bush administration two months after the start of the war, saying that the administration was "unwilling to come to grips" with the enormity of the postwar obligation in Iraq. "This is not what they were selling," White explained in a *USA Today* article on June 3, 2003.

The consequences exploded under U.S. forces. Bush's invasion was followed by widespread looting and anarchy. Insurgency quickly arose and continued to grow. Rough treatment of the civilian population and prisoners-of-war fueled anger. Civil strife fanned across the land.

While sufficient military forces may not have made the invasion of Iraq a "success," the failure to plan properly made it a true disaster. Establishing control through a larger force might have reduced postwar chaos; enabled the troops to disarm the sectarian militias; cool insurgency; protect electrical, health, and water facilities; and permit the country to revive. In any case, that is certainly not what happened.

The unrealistic expectations of Iraqis treating the U.S. military as saviors, coupled with Secretary Rumsfeld's experiments with the smallest possible military force and insistence on no "dependency" by the vanquished Iraqis, meant that the United States never properly established control. The consequences for our troops, our country, and the future are terrible.

President Bush had direct knowledge of the need for planning. Prime Minister Blair asked him about it before the invasion. The president reported that plans were in place.

He had signed off on plans, but they were deficient. The president ignored those who disagreed, and his administration punished others who challenged the low projections of troops needed to protect a country that is the size of California. After the occupation became a public disaster, he staunchly refused to remove or rebuke Secretary Rumsfeld, describing him as doing "a fine job."

General Anthony C. Zinni, once Bush's emissary to the region and the former leader of the Central Command for the Middle East, observed firsthand what he describes as a "lack of planning" for the postwar period. "I saw, at a minimum, true dereliction, negligence and irresponsibility," said Zinni.

As a result, war costs continue to rise. A report by the Congressional Research Service said in April 2006 that the costs are approaching $10 billion a month. In 2005 alone, costs reached $81 billion, according to the Center for Strategic and Budgetary Assessments, and are expected to hit $94 billion in 2006—outpacing the annual costs in Vietnam by more than $30 billion per year, even when adjusted to today's dollars.

The consequences in lost security are also harsh. Terrorist attacks worldwide tripled in 2005, reaching an all-time high of 11,000 incidents, killing 14,500 civilians (including police officers) and wounding 25,000, according to reports of the National Counterterrorism Center and the State Department released in April 2006. Experts pointed to Iraq as a significant cause. The State Department said Iraq had become a "pipeline" for international terrorists.

With U.S. resources and forces so occupied with Iraq, Osama bin Laden and his al Qaeda network still threaten to cause harm. Bin Laden continues to operate, inciting his followers to attack American civilians. Lieutenant General Gregory Newbold, former director of operations of the Joint Chiefs of Staff, who retired before the Iraq War, said the real menace is al Qaeda, not Iraq. "A fundamentally flawed plan was executed for an invented war [in Iraq], while pursuing the real enemy, Al Qaeda, became a secondary effort," Newbold said.

The president must be accountable for these acts. Thousands of U.S. soldiers have died or been severely injured in this postwar Iraq, as well as soldiers from Britain and other nations that joined the invasion. Many innocent Iraqis have suffered.

The recklessness and gross indifference to human life by President Bush in failing to "take care" in the planning for the postwar occupancy of Iraq is a high crime and misdemeanor that mandates his impeachment.

CONCLUSION: WHY IMPEACHMENT IS NECESSARY FOR THE PRESIDENT'S RECKLESS ENDANGERMENT OF HUMAN LIVES

These three areas—the failure to assume leadership during a national disaster; the failure to provide body armor for troops; the failure to plan for the postwar invasion of Iraq—

all demonstrate a reckless indifference to human lives by President Bush.

This reckless, wanton, and grossly negligent behavior has grave consequences for Americans, costing lives, health, and billions of dollars. These aspects of his failure to "take care" that the laws are faithfully executed are high crimes and misdemeanors for which the president should be impeached.

CHAPTER SEVEN

Impeachment for Leaking Classified Information

OVERVIEW

In July 2003, President Bush personally approved the leak of classified information in an attempt to deflect criticism of false statements he had made about Iraq's weapons of mass destruction. The leaked information consisted of selected portions of a highly classified document prepared nine months earlier—the October 2002 National Intelligence Estimate (NIE) on Iraq and weapons of mass destruction.

The leak of classified information from the NIE did not pertain to any national security purpose or, in fact, to any governmental need. The cut-and-paste selections released actually distorted the full picture in the NIE. The sole purpose of this endeavor was single-minded: to blunt charges coming from former Ambassador Joseph S. Wilson IV, notably in a *New York Times* op-ed, that cast doubt upon the veracity of the president's rationale for going to war.

In particular, Wilson challenged a statement made by the president in his 2003 State of the Union address that Iraq was trying to buy uranium for a nuclear bomb, a critical argument for going to war. Wilson had traveled to Niger to investigate the claim for the CIA in 2002 and reported it to be untrue. According to documents later filed in court, the White House went into a frenzy of activity in order to respond to Wilson.

The leak was a classic cover-up.

The NIE leak was intertwined with another leak—that of the identity of Valerie Plame, a covert CIA agent. Plame is married to Wilson. Because it can be damaging to national security, the intentional "outing" of a covert CIA employee is a potential violation of federal criminal law.

While serving as the district attorney of Brooklyn in the 1980s, I had to deal with sensitive issues surrounding undercover officers and their identities. Undercover police officers in Brooklyn took on risky and difficult assignments, trying to gather information on some of the most dangerous criminals. Blowing their cover endangers the lives of the officers, investigations are jeopardized, and public safety as a whole suffers.

Undercover CIA officers similarly work to cultivate sources and gather intelligence in the interest of national security. Plame worked on international issues related to weapons of mass destruction. Concerned for the safety of CIA officers and the integrity of its work, the CIA asked the Justice Department to investigate the "outing" of her identity.

In December 2003, Patrick Fitzgerald was named as a special prosecutor. In October 2005, a top aide to President Bush and Vice President Cheney, I. Lewis (Scooter) Libby, was identified as one of the people involved in passing Valerie Plame's name to reporters and was indicted for lying about his role to the grand jury and for obstruction of justice.

Information about the selective leak of the NIE came to light through the investigation of Plame's outing. As disclosed in court documents, Libby testified that the President Bush authorized the disclosure of parts of the classified NIE.

BACKGROUND: PRESIDENTIAL ABUSE OF POWER TO ATTACK ENEMIES

As the investigation into the leak of CIA Officer Plame unfolded, I saw, to my distress, some of the same techniques involved in Watergate: selective and misleading disclosures, misuse of government powers to damage political critics, and efforts to smear political opponents through criminal or quasi-criminal conduct. The use of covert retaliation seemed to be central themes in both situations. Like a bad remake of a bad movie, President Bush was engaging in the same bad behavior as President Nixon.

President Nixon used a variety of improper and abusive methods to attack his political adversaries. The "enemies' list" is one of the most notorious. Prominent individuals who opposed Nixon's policies, particularly Vietnam War objectors, suddenly found themselves targets of retaliation. President Nixon ordered the IRS to audit their taxes. These activities were an abuse of the power of his office and became one of the grounds for the impeachment vote against Nixon.

The Bush White House attack on Ambassador Wilson also echoes the Daniel Ellsberg affair, in which President Nixon wanted to smear Ellsberg after he leaked the Pentagon Papers. Nixon's object was to undermine the credibility of a Vietnam War critic, and his lackeys broke into the office of Ellsberg's psychiatrist to find "dirt."(See Chapter Two.) This became one of the grounds for the vote to impeach Nixon.

The Nixon White House engaged in criminal activity for the sole purpose of tarnishing a critic of the president's pursuit of a war; more than thirty years later, another White House appeared to be doing the same thing.

IMPEACHABLE OFFENSES IN THE BUSH LEAK MATTER

The president's ongoing efforts to mislead the public and Congress about his reasons for going to war in Iraq are distinct grounds for impeachment. (See Chapter Three.)

The leak of misleading portions of the classified NIE was an effort to cover up the president's deceptive statements during the State of the Union message and further deprive the American people of information with which to judge his actions.

The president has described the leak of the NIE as "declassification." The selective leaking—or declassification—of information for political purposes and not for legitimate government aims is an abuse of power. The fact is that whatever power is in the hands of the president must be used for the benefit of the nation and not to cover up a deceit, particularly about the reasons for going to war.

If the president's release of passages from the NIE is shown to be interlinked with the disclosure of a CIA agent's classified status or retaliation against a critic, this would be grave misconduct. Government officials, including the president, may not intentionally disclose the covert status of a federal employee, a clear endangerment to the employee, the employee's associates and contacts, and national security. The president may not cause harm to a federal employee in an act of personal retaliation against the person's spouse. The president may not condone, allow, or join in such an effort; to the contrary, the president must stop it.

If investigations reveal that President Bush knew of, authorized, or participated in an effort to reveal the identity of a covert CIA operative, then he has engaged in an egregious abuse of power. Such activity—a possible violation of the law and a breach of national security—constitutes a high crime and misdemeanor.

EVIDENCE AND DETAILS OF THE WHITE HOUSE LEAKS AND POSSIBLE PRESIDENTIAL INVOLVEMENT

In his January 28, 2003, State of the Union message, President Bush described his reasons for going to war. Key among them was the assertion that Saddam Hussein was building nuclear weapons. To support this claim, the president said,

"The British government has learned that Saddam Hussein recently sought significant quantities of uranium from Africa." (See Chapter Three.)

In the weeks and months after the March 19, 2003, invasion of Iraq, no weapons of mass destruction were uncovered. Questions increasingly arose about the credibility of the president's prewar statements. Former Ambassador Joe Wilson began to criticize Bush to journalists in May 2003.

In a July 6, 2003, opinion-editorial in the *New York Times* titled "What I Didn't Find in Africa," Wilson wrote that intelligence had been "twisted to exaggerate the Iraqi threat." He specifically referred to President Bush's claim in his State of the Union address that Saddam was seeking uranium.

Wilson had a solid basis to challenge the uranium claim. At the request of the CIA, he had traveled to Niger in February 2002 to investigate the very question of whether Iraq had sought uranium. He found that it was not true.

The original suspicion that Saddam might be seeking uranium in Niger was based on a document dated in 2000 and that first surfaced in France and Italy in 2001. It purported to show that Iraq was buying five hundred tons of high-quality yellowcake uranium to build a nuclear bomb. The document was quickly discredited by European intelligence agencies as a crass forgery—it had misspellings, was on stolen stationery, and purported to carry the signature of a Niger official no longer in office on the date of the document.

But in 2002 Vice President Cheney asked the CIA to check out the claim that Iraq was attempting to purchase uranium from Niger. The agency sent Wilson. Wilson, who had served in the region and was very familiar with key players, had a formidable resume—chargé d'affaires in Baghdad prior to the Persian Gulf War in 1991, ambassador to Africa under the first President Bush, part of African planning on the National Security Council under President Clinton. He wasn't on the CIA staff but had agreed to similar missions in the past, and he agreed again.

After spending eight days in Niger, Wilson had the answer for the CIA. "It did not take long to conclude that it was highly doubtful that any such transaction had ever taken place," he wrote in the *Times*. He reported his findings back to the CIA in March 2002. Before the Iraq War began, two other high-level government officials separately reached the same conclusion—the U.S. ambassador to Niger and a four-star Marine Corps general. There was no disagreement on this point.

By writing the op-ed in July 2003 and going public with his findings, Wilson pointed to the president as wrong on a vital fact. More important, he exposed the president as lying and said President Bush was taking the United States to war under "false pretenses." The timing came at a critical juncture. Now that the United States had occupied Iraq for two months, Americans were trying to understand the failure to uncover any weapons of mass destruction—the threat had been portrayed as so enormous and imminent in the run-up to the war.

Wilson wrote that he felt confident from years of government experience that Vice President Cheney had been

informed personally and before the war of his findings that
the uranium claim was false. Yet, the vice president had
firmly—and deceptively—reaffirmed the uranium claim on
television just three days before the invasion of Iraq. When
asked on *Meet the Press* about a different report that the uranium claim was a fake—by Mohamed ElBaradei, director of
the International Atomic Energy Agency—Cheney said, "Mr.
ElBaradei frankly is wrong."

The July 2003 op-ed by Wilson posed a particularly serious
threat to President Bush by reopening charges of presidential
deception.

The White House developed a two-part response. First, it
would show that U.S. intelligence agencies gave the president
false information about the Niger uranium purchase. In that
way, blame for the untrue "sixteen words" in the State of the
Union address could be shifted from the president to the CIA
or others. Clearly, if the president relied on incorrect intelligence reports, then he didn't lie.

In Watergate parlance, this tactic was a "modified limited
hang-out," a term made up by Nixon aide John Ehrlichman
to describe a scheme to protect President Nixon from allegations of wrongdoing. The plan in Watergate was for the
White House to issue a report that would claim a thorough
investigation and exonerate the president and his staff.

In President Bush's case, the idea involved releasing snip-
pets from the NIE but leaving the rest classified. According
to grand jury testimony by Libby, the president specifically
authorized him to leak to reporters a portion of the NIE. The

portion, in isolation, might seem to provide a basis for the false sixteen words about uranium.

But this leak itself was a form of disinformation. Even though in April 2006, when the leak was exposed, the president stated that he authorized selective "declassification" because he "wanted people to see the truth," in fact the chosen passages were designed to mislead and confuse.

The NIE coordinates the opinions of six intelligence agencies and sets out minority opinions and when they exist, a consensus opinion. The majority of the intelligence agencies (five out of six) held that the uranium story could not be confirmed and had been disproven. The leaked portion of the NIE reflected the minority position of a single agency (not the CIA) which said Iraq was attempting to procure uranium and that the status of the Niger deal was unknown. What was not leaked included a special alert by the State Department's intelligence division that the uranium allegation was "highly dubious." In total, this leak distorted the thrust of the NIE.

Libby said he was also instructed to describe some of the key judgments in the document and to say that it stated Iraq was "vigorously" trying to procure uranium. In the actual document, the uranium claim was not a "key judgment"—a signpost of importance—because it had been so strongly contested that it had been downgraded in importance.

At the time of the president's State of the Union address, the White House knew from many sources, in addition to Wilson's report, that the Niger uranium claim was untrue. The CIA had debunked the Niger claim—more than once—

and told the White House of its falsity. So had other intelligence agencies. (See Chapter Three.)

When Wilson's op-ed finally ripped the cover off the false uranium claim, the president shifted responsibility to the CIA. President Bush issued a statement while on a trip to Africa on July 7, 2003, that the "sixteen words" on uranium should not have been in his State of the Union address. On that same day in Washington, CIA Director Tenet said it was his blunder. When the press pointed to prior CIA warnings, Deputy National Security Advisor Stephen Hadley said the sixteen words were his fault.

The second element of the White House effort to switch the focus away from the president's deceptive statement was to attack Wilson, the messenger who revealed the "twisted" intelligence.

From May through July 2003, the White House collected substantial information about Wilson, according to information in the later indictment of Libby. This included his wife's status as a covert agent in the CIA counterinsurgency division.

Libby, who bore the titles of assistant to the president for national security affairs, assistant to the vice president for national security affairs, and chief of staff for the vice president, disclosed that Wilson's wife was a CIA covert employee in a meeting with Judith Miller of the *New York Times* on June 23, 2003, according the indictment filed by the special prosecutor in October 2005. One purpose in mentioning Plame was to portray Wilson's trip as a junket arrranged by his wife and not a serious mission.

On July 8, 2003, Libby met again with Miller and, at this meeting, shared the distorted NIE material and, again, the fact that Wilson's wife was a covert employee of CIA. Libby said in grand jury testimony that the vice president "specifically directed" him to disclose key portions of the NIE. Libby wanted the president's approval, too. Vice President Cheney then sought and secured the president's approval, Libby testified.

According to court documents filed by Special Prosecutor Fitzgerald, "[Libby] testified that the vice president later advised him that the president had authorized defendant [Libby] to disclose the relevant portions of the NIE." Libby also talked to the legal counsel to the vice president, who indicated that the president's permission to disclose the NIE "amounted to a declassification" of the document. Special Prosecutor Fitzgerald later said in a court document that only three people knew that the NIE had been "declassified"—the president, the vice president, and Libby. Even other White House officials were unaware of the goings-on.

When Libby gave the information about Wilson's wife to Miller, he asked to be anonymous and to be described as a "former Hill staffer." A story by Miller was not published.

The first public disclosure of Valerie Plame's CIA status came in a column by conservative pundit Robert Novak on July 14, 2003. He said his information came from "two senior administration officials." Later, it became apparent that a handful of other reporters received the same information from people inside the White House.

Because the outing of a covert CIA employee may be a

federal crime, the CIA asked the Justice Department to investigate. Attorney General John Ashcroft eventually determined that he had a conflict of interest because of his close ties to the president's political adviser, Karl Rove.

Fitzgerald, a career federal prosecutor, was named special prosecutor on December 30, 2003, with the assignment "to investigate the alleged unauthorized disclosure of a CIA employee's identity." Following nearly two years of investigation, including interviews of dozens of people and the jailing of one reporter (Miller) for refusing to divulge her sources, on October 28, 2005, Libby was indicted on five counts of perjury, obstruction of justice, and other federal crimes. The indictment alleged that Libby released Valerie Plame's identity on multiple occasions and to several reporters and that he was dishonest about it when questioned before the grand jury. A trial is scheduled for early 2007. Fitzgerald continued to investigate the case as of the end of June 2006.

In a press conference about the Libby indictment, Fitzgerald underscored the importance of protecting CIA identities: "It's important that a CIA officer's identity be protected . . . not just for the officer but for the nation's security. . . . The damage wasn't to one person. It wasn't to Valerie Wilson, it was done to all of us," he said. "This is a very serious matter and compromising national security information is a very serious matter. . . . And we need to know the truth."

Fitzgerald also stated in documents filed in court in April 2006 that Wilson's op-ed "was viewed in the office of the vice president as a direct attack on the credibility of the vice president and the president." There was, said Fitzgerald, "concerted action" by "multiple people in the White House" to "discredit, punish or seek revenge against" Wilson.

Wilson suspected as much. At one point, he received a call from TV talk-host Chris Matthews, who repeated a conversation with Rove, the White House political advisor, who reportedly said, "Wilson's wife is fair game." The White House may well have known that hurting the career of Wilson's wife by revealing her CIA identity would be an especially painful form of retaliation against Wilson. At the same time, it would send a clear signal to any other would-be critics of the president of the kind of reprisals they could expect.

The White House did not deny that the president was involved in leaking—or declassifying, a spokesperson said—portions of the NIE. The president admitted it, as well. In an April 10, 2006, forum at The John Hopkins School of Advanced International Studies, he said that he had authorized the release of information in the highly classified NIE. Fitzgerald said in a court filing that he believes the president was "unaware" that Libby was disclosing Plame's name.

However, both leaks—one of classified material and the other of a classified identity—were connected. And the two had the same objectives: to undermine Wilson and to cover up for the president's false statements about the war.

The first person to leak Valerie Plame's identity, columnist Novak, said in a speech in December 2005 that the president knows who leaked it to him. "I'm confident the president knows who the source is," Novak said to a luncheon gathering

in North Carolina, according to the *Raleigh News &
Observer.* "So I say, don't bug me. . . . Bug the president."

CONCLUSION: WHY IMPEACHMENT
MAY BE NECESSARY FOR LEAKING
CLASSIFIED INFORMATION

Knowing the president's exact role in the "outing" of Valerie
Plame is essential to determining whether his conduct constitutes an impeachable offense.

This is not solely in the province of the special prosecutor,
as important as his investigation is. Congress must also conduct a serious investigation. The president should come clean
and answer what he knew and when he knew it with respect
to the outing of Valerie Plame. The president should make
public the statements he made to the special prosecutor in
conjunction with the investigation. If the president made
false statements to investigators, as Libby is charged with
doing, the president could be guilty of a crime.

The president should answer when and why he authorized a
selective leak of material from the NIE. The full ninety-six-page
NIE still has not been declassified. (There are other questions
for the president that relate to his knowledge of the uranium
claim itself. The issue is not how the sixteen words got into the
president's speech, but what the president knew, or should
have known, about the falseness of the uranium claim itself.)

The leak of the NIE, an attempt to create a distorted picture of the information available to the president when he was
making a case for war, is an abuse of power. It was not leaked

for purposes related to legitimate government needs. Taken on its own, this conduct might not rise to the level of an impeachable offense. If, however, the leak of the NIE were part of a broader campaign to use the powers of the office to silence a critic, impeachment may be appropriate.

The president and vice president should be questioned about documents in their possession or control relating to the disclosure of Plame's identity as a CIA agent. In a federal court hearing in Washington in February 2006, lawyers on the case described 250 pages of e-mails from the office of the vice president that were belatedly turned over, many months after the special prosecutor sought them. Only weeks earlier, the special prosecutor had reported that the White House said the e-mails had not been preserved or archived "in the normal process" and were not available.

The loss of e-mails might be the updated equivalent of President Nixon's attempt to cover up his misdeeds by withholding and altering tapes from his White House recording system. The famous eighteen and one-half minute gap cut out the voices on one crucial tape—his longtime secretary said she accidentally hit the wrong button while transcribing it. The Supreme Court finally ordered Nixon to turn over all of the tapes sought by the special prosecutor and, when his role in orchestrating the cover-up of Watergate became indisputably clear, Nixon resigned. Vice President Cheney, President Bush, and their staffs must be questioned by Congress about how e-mails were misarchived, and what, if any, remain to be recovered or released. Deliberately withholding evidence from investigators is obstruction of justice and a basis for impeachment.

President Bush's selective declassification of information in an effort to cover up his own deceit is an abuse of power. If he is further involved in the disclosure of a covert CIA agent, a breach of national security, impeachment is warranted.

CHAPTER EIGHT

Impeachment and Vice President Cheney

ROLES OF THE PRESIDENT AND VICE PRESIDENT

The Constitution specifically provides for the impeachment of the vice president. As with a president, the grounds on which a vice president may be removed from office are "treason, bribery or other high crimes and misdemeanors."

Lurking in the background of the impeachment of President Bush is the question of Vice President Dick Cheney. Why should impeachment focus on the president and not on the vice president? Various commentators say if the president is removed, Cheney will step into the Oval Office, and he is just as bad or worse. Undoubtedly, Cheney has been involved in many of the same impeachable offenses as the president.

The first impeachment effort, some say, should remove the vice president.

They are wrong.

Impeachment of President Bush serves two purposes. First and most important, the impeachment will assert a bedrock value of the country that no one is above the law. Impeachment of President Bush aims directly at a president who believes and acts otherwise.

Second, impeachment will remove from office a president who threatens our liberties with repeated and serious violations of the Constitution.

A lawless president cannot be allowed to remain in office.

Other powerful reasons dictate why President Bush should be the first subject of impeachment rather than the vice president.

President Bush describes himself as the "decider." Constitutionally, the president holds the reins of power. He is responsible for the impeachable offenses described in this book. The buck stops there, to paraphrase President Truman.

EVIDENCE OF CHENEY'S IMPEACHABLE OFFENSES

Evidence for the impeachment of President Bush is strong and compelling, ranging from his multiple deceptions and falsehoods to take the country to war in Iraq to his authorization of domestic wiretaps in violation of the law; from his condoning of abusive treatment of war prisoners to his utter indifference to the impending loss of life in the Hurricane Katrina disaster, and more.

While Vice President Cheney has played an unusual role for a vice president in the formulation and execution of policy, we do not see his fingerprints on every high crime and misdemeanor that involves the president.

In the case of the failure to deliver emergency resources and disaster assistance to the Gulf Coast during Hurricane Katrina (see Chapter Six),the president is the one who listened to a briefing about the catastrophe bearing down on New Orleans, and then carried on with his August vacation. The president, and the president alone, had the power to activate a massive federal emergency response. The vice president's hand is not apparent (although he, too, vacationed through Katrina).

In the matter of the warrantless domestic wiretaps, President Bush explicitly authorized and reauthorized the activities in defiance of the FISA law. (See Chapter Four.) He admits to this. He signed executive orders at least thirty times—one every forty-five days—permitting warrantless surveillance without the approval of Congress or the courts. The president has expressly contravened a federal law and said that he plans to continue to do so.

The vice president is a supporter and advocate of the wireless wiretapping program. When the secret program was exposed, he went on *Nightline* in December 2005 and invoked, sensationally, the terror of 9/11. He declared, without one shred of evidence, that the illegal wiretapping "might well have been able to stop it." According to a May 2006 *New York Times* article, Vice President Cheney and his legal advisor took an aggressive view of surveillance and pushed the National Security Agency to bend the rules and secretly collect the call-logs of Americans without the permission of Congress or the courts. But, at this point, evidence of his participation is secondhand.

The imprint of the vice president is not nearly so visible as the president's on the issue of torture and the cruel and degrading treatment of war detainees. (See Chapter Five.) While key legal opinions circulated to the office of the vice president, such as one claiming that the president may override the antitorture laws, the vice president did not sign the key February 7 document derailing the Geneva Conventions. The president did. Still, the vice president and his close aide David Addington participated in back-and-forth discussions of the Bush military detention policies, according to *New Yorker* writer Jane Mayer. Colonel Larry Wilkerson, an aide to Secretary of State Colin Powell, said he prepared an "audit trail" of torture reports and found that they led directly to the office of the vice president, although, at present, this evidence is hearsay.

The vice president lobbied Congress to defeat antitorture legislation introduced by Senator John McCain and to exclude the CIA from its coverage. But once the legislation passed, the president is the one who put ink to a "signing statement" that purports to let him nullify the law. Vice President Cheney's role is opaque.

On the issue of reckless indifference to human life in failing to provide body armor for troops and failing to plan for the postwar occupation in Iraq (see Chapter Six), the president is responsible as commander in chief. By all accounts, the vice president, a former defense secretary, was deeply involved in the Iraq War planning. But the vice president has no formal place in the chain of military command.

We do know that Vice President Cheney favors the concept of an imperial president. He opposes post-Watergate and post–Vietnam War restraints on presidential powers. But ideas alone are not cause for impeachment.

In two interconnected areas, the vice president's role is unmistakable.

In the run-up to the war in Iraq, Cheney joined fully as a mouthpiece of misrepresentation. (See Chapter Three.) Vice President Cheney frequently used his position to make statements about the war that were false. He paraded the phony weapons of mass destruction claims and said that he knew with certainty that Iraq was reconstituting its nuclear program, a falsehood. In August 2002, Cheney said, "Many of us are concerned that Saddam Hussein will acquire nuclear weapons fairly soon." Cheney said it was "as grave a threat as can be imagined."

Cheney continued to assert that Saddam was linked to 9/11, repeatedly pointing to a supposed meeting in Prague between 9/11 hijacker Mohammed Atta and an Iraqi agent, even after U.S. intelligence officials determined that Atta was in Virginia at the time. Cheney insisted that no one could prove that the meeting hadn't happened.

President Bush, like Cheney, made many misleading and deceptive statements to the public. But President Bush also signed a "letter of determination" to Congress, declaring, untruthfully, that the invasion of Iraq met congressionally mandated requirements and conditions on military action.

The vice president was a central force in duping the American people and taking the country to war in Iraq based on untruths. If he participated in this attack on our democracy knowing the falsity of statements, he would be guilty of high crimes and misdemeanors. The circumstances suggest that the vice president was fully knowledgeable; further investigation would clarify his role.

In a second area, Vice President Cheney was also intricately involved. He aided in the July 2003 leak of classified national security information. (See Chapter Seven.) The leak had nothing to do with a legitimate governmental purpose; one of its aims was to cover up for deceptions made by the vice president, as well as the president, to induce the country to go to war in Iraq.

The leaked document distorted the truth and was intended to contradict a war critic, former Ambassador Joseph Wilson, who had directly attacked the vice president for his prewar statements. (Wilson had also challenged the president for his State of the Union address.) Wilson said that the vice president knew before the war of the falsity of the claim that Iraq was buying uranium for nuclear weapons but that he deceptively repeated this claim to urge military action. Wilson pointed to Cheney's comment on *Meet the Press* three days before the U.S. invasion of Iraq. There, Cheney insisted again that the uranium claim was true and dismissing the findings of the UN inspectors to the contrary.

The leak of classified documents occurred at the same time as the outing of a covert CIA agent, Valerie Plame, who was married to Wilson—a possible crime.

Cheney's chief of staff, I. Lewis (Scooter) Libby, has been indicted on five counts of lying and obstruction of justice. According to grand jury testimony by Libby described in court papers, the vice president "specifically directed" him to leak the classified document. Whether and how the vice president was involved in outing the CIA agent is unclear at this point. If the vice president personally knew of, directed, or authorized the disclosure of the CIA agent's identity, he would be impeachable on those grounds.

CONCLUSION: WHY IMPEACHMENT OF THE PRESIDENT PRECEDES IMPEACHMENT OF THE VICE PRESIDENT

In the end, the president is responsible for the impeachable offenses described in this book, and it is he who should be held accountable.

During the course of the inquiry conducted in connection with the impeachment of President Bush, it is likely that additional evidence will emerge about what the vice president knew, when he knew it, and how he used what he knew.

But it would be wrong to wait until that happens. Impeachment is a strategy to uphold the Constitution, not to weigh political advantage. Our democracy depends on our stopping the frightening abuse of power by the president, and future presidents must know they cannot subvert the Constitution.

So, the focus is properly placed on first removing President Bush for his many impeachable offenses. And if the president is impeached and the vice president does not have the good sense to pack his bags, then impeachment proceedings can begin against him, as well.

CHAPTER NINE

What You Can Do

How does the process of impeachment of George W. Bush start?
"Enough."

Americans have to say "enough."

It's that simple. It starts on any day, after any piece of news. It comes after another soldier's death, another intrusion into private lives with illegal domestic spying, another grab for power from the White House. It comes when people say no more to lawbreaking from the president.

Of course, there are constitutional components and legislative intricacies and evidentiary questions to maneuver. This process begins in earnest when the House of Representatives directs the House Judiciary Committee to commence an impeachment inquiry, as happened in Nixon's case.

But the real process of impeachment begins with the American people.

In the case of President Nixon and the Watergate scandals, people finally demanded that the House of Representatives take action against a president who placed himself above the law. Impeachment had been discussed for months; an impeachment resolution had even been introduced in the summer of 1973, but was ignored. Finally, when President Nixon had the Watergate special prosecutor fired, people across the country flooded their representatives with letters and phone calls, demanding action. The clamor grew, and it didn't go away. The House was forced to respond; it authorized the impeachment inquiry to begin.

With President Bush, more and more people have reached a boiling point. Evidence of his abuses of power and failures to execute the law has mounted, and an understanding of the necessity for impeachment is growing. At forums across the country and in online communities, people are coming together to try to make it happen. It is possible.

Here are some ideas about how to mobilize support for the impeachment of George W. Bush:

1. *Gear up.* Inform yourself and your friends about impeachment—understand what the Constitution provides and what the president has done that requires his removal. Host a discussion in your home, dorm, or favorite local spot. Play some music—"Let's Impeach the

President" from Neil Young's *Living with War* CD is a good one to get the evening rolling. Make a handout, explaining that impeachment is a way to remove someone from office, and listing the top reasons to do so. More information is available at the Web site for this book, www.ImpeachBushBook.com.

2. *Reach out.* Grassroots organizing is essential. Contact local political clubs, veterans' groups, and organizations that support freedom of speech, civil liberties, and peace activism. See if you can make a presentation to the group. Ask them to endorse impeachment and to pass materials to their networks. Get in touch with online organization efforts, such as Afterdowningstreet.com, Impeachpac.com, and Impeachbush.tv. Take fliers to street fairs, state fairs, lemonade stands, and gas stations (the price on the pump helps focus people in an important way). Impeachment is for everyone—don't be afraid to reach out to moderates and others who may have supported Bush in the past, and explain why you are working to save our democracy.

3. *Speak out.* Call your local talk radio station. Write letters to local press and television. Make a petition, calling for impeachment, and present it to your colleagues and friends. Post a statement on your Web site or blog, and make comments on political blogs such as DailyKos. Sponsor a forum at your town hall, community center, or public park. Make a small business-sized card with reasons

for impeachment, and direct people to more information on a Web site with impeachment information.

4. *Meet reps.* Impeachment formally starts in the U.S. House of Representatives, so make sure your representative hears why you think it's important. Help representatives understand what you've learned about the process of impeachment and the issues involved by providing the kind of literature and information contained in this book. Some congressional representatives need a lot of support to bolster their courage and do the right thing. Write, call, e-mail. Get your friends to do the same. Especially, try to meet with your representatives—they have to be elected every two years, and elections years are big years for them.

Ask your representative to sponsor a hearing on one of the issues in this book that will form the basis for impeachment—deceptions leading to the war, permitting torture, violation of laws on wiretapping, failure to respond to Katrina, and others.

Get your representative to commit to signing House Resolution 635 (109th Congress), introduced by U.S. Representative John Conyers, Jr. of Michigan, calling for an inquiry into whether impeachment is warranted. It's a first step, from which the next step—a full inquiry into impeachment—can be taken. By summer 2006, thirty-seven representatives had signed up; more are needed. The resolution calls for "Creating a select committee to investigate the

Administration's intent to go to war before congressional authorization, manipulation of pre-war intelligence, encouraging and countenancing torture, retaliating against critics, and to make recommendations regarding grounds for possible impeachment." Send a little thank you note to Rep. Conyers, too, for standing up for our rights.

Contact your senators, as well. And, while you are at it, get in touch with the majority leader and the minority leader in the House of Representatives; they need to understand that people want impeachment to move forward.

5. *Go statewide, go local.* State and local elective bodies can pass resolutions that represent the community's collective voice. They draw public attention, raise awareness, and create pressure on Congresspersons to act.

State resolutions of impeachment voted by a state legislature go directly to the House of Representatives. This is a way to trigger action in the House, but there's a catch.

Normally, an impeachment resolution must be introduced by a member of the House. A special introduction is mentioned in a manual of rules for the House, first written in 1801 by Thomas Jefferson ("Jefferson's Manual"). It has this sentence: "There are several methods of setting an impeachment in motion . . . [one of them is] by charges transmitted from the legislatures of States" (Section 603). The catch is that once the state resolution is "transmitted" to the House, it can be ignored.

Still, state resolutions have enormous value in raising the consciousness of the American people and in describing the grounds for impeachment. By summer 2006, resolutions had been introduced in California, Illinois, and Vermont—states with combined populations of 50 million or 16 percent of the nation's people.

Local resolutions also can be a wake-up call from constituents. City and local town boards are approachable in many locations, and a few dedicated people can make something happen. By summer 2006, resolutions calling for the impeachment of President Bush had been passed in more than a dozen cities and towns, including Arcata, California; Newfane, Vermont; Plattsburg, New York; Nederland, Colorado; Chapel Hill, North Carolina; and San Francisco (Board of Supervisors), California. They are a way to get the ball rolling.

6. *Vote nationally.* Key congressional races across the country can make a difference, and you can make a difference in them. It's critical to elect representatives who will support impeachment, or at least keep an open mind. The present Congress has refused to support investigations into the serious misconduct of President Bush. Our democracy is being gutted, but many representatives and senators are standing idle. They can be replaced. Where an obstinate incumbent is beatable, you can support the challenger through volunteer help and contributions, no matter where you live. Getting the right members in

Congress is as important now as the next presidential ticket. We need a Congress willing to take action, and we can put it in place.

7. *Keep going.* Impeachment of George W. Bush won't be easy, and it won't happen without fortitude and determination. Even with new faces in the House and Senate, pressure from the public will be critical to get the Congress to act. Don't be discouraged. No one can predict what will happen. The only thing that is certain, as far as impeachment is concerned, is that it won't happen at all if people don't mobilize and take action. We learned from the presidency of Richard M. Nixon, and now of George W. Bush, that officials who feel entitled to abuse power won't stop unless the people stop them. The movement for impeachment of President Bush is the right thing to do to preserve our democracy.

CHAPTER TEN

Why Impeachment Is Necessary

The grounds for the impeachment of George W. Bush are grave, serious, and multiple.

Like President Nixon, President Bush has conducted a far-reaching assault on our constitutional system. The menace to our democracy is great and growing.

The cure for constitutional crimes of this magnitude is to impeach President Bush and remove him from office. Our Constitution's framers gave us the remedy for exactly this kind of brazen attack.

Previously in the nation's history—during Watergate—we had to preserve the rule of law from a president who seriously abused his powers. Skeptics, antagonists, and defeatists argued then against impeachment of President Nixon. But action was necessary to preserve our system. Impeachment was the right thing to do, and the country was better for it.

Today, some will ask again: What are the chances? Why bother? How can a drive to impeach possibly succeed?

But our democracy can only survive if the people it serves are willing to fight for it. Who else will save our democracy, if not us? How else can people act, if they care deeply about freedom and liberty? We simply cannot sit by, paralyzed or impassive, while our freedoms are dismantled piece-by-piece.

The heroes in our nation's history who fought for liberty never calculated the odds. They just did what was right, and the legacy of their heroism is all around us. We had patriots who overthrew the yoke of George III in the Revolutionary War. We had suffragists who insisted that women were entitled to equality at the voting booth. We had civil rights advocates who demanded an end to segregation. We had civilians and soldiers and students and professors who said no to the Vietnam War. They didn't stop to ask whether they could really succeed; they just stood up against injustice because there was no other alternative. And they succeeded.

When the impeachment process against Richard Nixon began, no one could fully predict what would happen. Members of the Judiciary Committee during Watergate tried to do the right thing in the right way. We didn't know what all the evidence would show, or that President Nixon would resign; we only knew that preserving our democracy required a thorough investigation of his abuses of power.

I was proud to serve on the Judiciary Committee. My mother and her parents fled from the Ukraine in 1921 in the face of a communist dictatorship that was tightening its dark grip on the population. They came to America for freedom. I know from their stories that I cannot take our liberties for granted.

If anything, the urgency of impeachment is increasing. Major and worrisome disclosures unfold on a weekly basis.

Boston Globe writer Charlie Savage reported in late April 2006 that the president has filed official statements saying that he is not bound to obey 750 bills that he signed into law. They include protections for federal whistleblowers, a prohibition on sending U.S. troops into combat in Columbia, reports on the vulnerability of chemical plants to terrorism, and implementation of affirmative action.

This is a grotesque violation of his oath of office and his job. President Bush has taken the extraordinary position that he is not obliged to enforce laws that he doesn't feel like enforcing. Under the Constitution, the president must execute all the laws, not just the ones he likes or approves of. And he must obey all the laws, not just the ones that suit him.

How many other laws, of the thousands on the books, does he also feel free to disobey?

We don't know what further revelations of presidential misconduct and impeachable offenses are left to be uncovered. What we know now is frightening; it is enough.

All of the evidence shows that President Bush, if he remains in office, will continue to be a threat to our liberties and the rule of law. And if the effort to remove him does not succeed, at least we will not be found wanting for failing to try.

In a democracy the people have the power to control the destiny of the country. In the end, the responsibility is on our shoulders. Democracy is a gift that was handed to us by the generations that came before us; we should not pass it on to a new generation in a shrunken state. To preserve our constitutional system, impeachment is necessary—now.

APPENDICES

A-(i) Constitutional Provisions on Impeachment; (ii) Excerpt from the Debates on Impeachment from the Constitutional Convention, 1787

B-Constitutional Provisions on Presidential Responsibilities and War Powers

C-Constitutional Provisions on Congress's War Powers

D-Excerpts from the Bill of Rights – Fourth, Fifth, Eighth Amendments

E-Articles of Impeachment Against Richard M. Nixon, Adopted

F-Article of Impeachment Against Richard M. Nixon on Cambodia, *Not Adopted*

G-Excerpts from Opinion of Justice Jackson, U.S. Supreme Court, on Presidential Powers, *The Steel Seizure Case*

H-Excerpts from the Geneva Conventions

Appendix A
(i) Constitutional Provisions on Impeachment

Article I, Section 2

The House of Representatives . . . shall have the sole Power of Impeachment.

Article I, Section 3

The Senate shall have the sole Power to try all Impeachments. When sitting for that Purpose, they shall be on Oath or Affirmation. When the President of the United States is tried, the Chief Justice shall preside: And no Person shall be convicted without the concurrence of two thirds of the Members present.

Judgment in Cases of Impeachment shall not extend further than to removal from Office, and disqualification to hold and enjoy any Office of honor, Trust or Profit under the United States; but the Party convicted shall nevertheless be liable and subject to Indictment, Trial, Judgment and Punishment, according to Law.

Article II, Section 4

The President, Vice President and all civil Officers of the United States, shall be removed from Office on Impeachment for, and Conviction of, Treason, Bribery, or other high Crimes and Misdemeanors.

Appendix A
(ii) Constitutional Convention Debates on Impeachment, Excerpt from Max Farrand's *The Records of the Federal Convention of 1787*, Vol. 2, p. 550.

The clause referring to . . . the trial of impeachments agst. the President, for Treason & bribery, was taken up.

Col. Mason. Why is the provision restrained to Treason & bribery only? Treason as defined in the Constitution will not reach many great and dangerous offences. . . . Attempts to subvert the Constitution may not be Treason as above defined— . . . He movd. to add after "bribery" "or maladministration" Mr. Gerry seconded him—

Mr Madison So vague a term will be equivalent to a tenure during pleasure of the Senate.

Mr Govr Morris, it will not be put in force & can do no harm— An election of every four years will prevent maladministration.

Col. Mason withdrew "maladministration" & substitutes "other high crimes & misdemeanors" <agst. the State">

On the question thus altered N. H— ay. Mas. ay— Ct. ay. <N. J. no> Pa no. Del. no. Md ay. Va. ay. N. C. ay. S. C. ay. Geo. ay. [Ayes — 8; noes — 3.]

Appendix B
Constitutional Provisions on Presidential Responsibilities and War Powers

Oath of Office

Article II, Section 1, Clause 7 of the Constitution

I do solemnly swear that I will faithfully execute the Office of the President of the United States, and will to the best of my ability, preserve, protect and defend the Constitution of the United States.

Presidential Responsibilities

Article II, Section 3

[The President] . . . shall take Care that the Laws be faithfully executed ...

Presidential War Powers

Article II, Section 2

The President shall be Commander in Chief of the Army and Navy of the United States, and of the Militia of the several States, when called into the actual Service of the United States.

Appendix C
Constitutional Provisions Congress's War Powers

Article I, Section 8

The Congress shall have Power To . . . provide for the common Defence . . . ;

To define and punish Piracies and Felonies committed on the high Seas, and Offences against the Law of Nations;

To declare War, grant Letters of Marque and Reprisal, and make Rules concerning Captures on Land and Water;

To raise and support Armies, but no Appropriation of Money to that Use shall be for a longer Term than two Years;

To provide and maintain a Navy;

To make Rules for the Government and Regulation of the land and naval Forces;

To provide for calling forth the Militia to execute the Laws of the Union, suppress Insurrections and repeal Invasions;

To provide for organizing, arming, and disciplining the Militia, and for governing such Part of them as may be employed in the Service of the United States, reserving to the States respectively, the Appointment of the Officers, and the Authority of training the Militia according to the discipline prescribed by Congress; . . .

To make all Laws which shall be necessary and proper for carrying into Execution the foregoing Powers, and all other Powers vested by this Constitution in the Government of the United States, or in any Department or Officer thereof.

Appendix D
Excerpts from the Bill of Rights

Fourth Amendment
The right of the people to be secure in their persons, houses, papers, and effects, against unreasonable searches and seizures, shall not be violated, and no Warrants shall issue, but upon probable cause, supported by Oath or affirmation, and particularly describing the place to be searched, and the persons or things to be seized.

Fifth Amendment
No person . . . shall be compelled in any criminal case to be a witness against himself, nor be deprived of life, liberty, or property, without due process of law.

Eighth Amendment

Excessive bail shall not be required, nor excessive fines imposed, nor cruel and unusual punishments inflicted.

Appendix E

Adopted Articles of Impeachment against Richard M. Nixon

Articles of Impeachment of Richard M. Nixon
Adopted by the Committee on the Judiciary July 27–30, 1974

Article 1

RESOLVED, That Richard M. Nixon, President of the United States, is impeached for high crimes and misdemeanors, and that the following articles of impeachment to be exhibited to the Senate:

ARTICLES OF IMPEACHMENT EXHIBITED BY THE HOUSE OF REPRESENTATIVES OF THE UNITED STATES OF AMERICA IN THE NAME OF ITSELF AND OF ALL OF THE PEOPLE OF THE UNITED STATES OF AMERICA, AGAINST RICHARD M. NIXON, PRESIDENT OF THE UNITED STATES OF AMERICA, IN MAINTENANCE AND SUPPORT OF ITS IMPEACHMENT AGAINST HIM FOR HIGH CRIMES AND MISDEMEANORS.

ARTICLE 1
In his conduct of the office of President of the United States,

Richard M. Nixon, in violation of his constitutional oath faithfully to execute the office of President of the United States and, to the best of his ability, preserve, protect, and defend the Constitution of the United States, and in violation of his constitutional duty to take care that the laws be faithfully executed, has prevented, obstructed, and impeded the administration of justice, in that:

On June 17, 1972, and prior thereto, agents of the Committee for the Re-election of the President committed unlawful entry of the headquarters of the Democratic National Committee in Washington, District of Columbia, for the purpose of securing political intelligence. Subsequent thereto, Richard M. Nixon, using the powers of his high office, engaged personally and through his close subordinates and agents, in a course of conduct or plan designed to delay, impede, and obstruct the investigation of such illegal entry; to cover up, conceal and protect those responsible; and to conceal the existence and scope of other unlawful covert activities.

The means used to implement this course of conduct or plan included one or more of the following:

1. making false or misleading statements to lawfully authorized investigative officers and employees of the United States;

2. withholding relevant and material evidence or information

from lawfully authorized investigative officers and employees of the United States;

3. approving, condoning, acquiescing in, and counseling witnesses with respect to the giving of false or misleading statements to lawfully authorized investigative officers and employees of the United States and false or misleading testimony in duly instituted judicial and congressional proceedings;

4. interfering or endeavoring to interfere with the conduct of investigations by the Department of Justice of the United States, the Federal Bureau of Investigation, the office of Watergate Special Prosecution Force, and Congressional Committees;

5. approving, condoning, and acquiescing in, the surreptitious payment of substantial sums of money for the purpose of obtaining the silence or influencing the testimony of witnesses, potential witnesses or individuals who participated in such unlawful entry and other illegal activities;

6. endeavoring to misuse the Central Intelligence Agency, an agency of the United States;

7. disseminating information received from officers of the Department of Justice of the United States to subjects of investigations conducted by lawfully authorized

investigative officers and employees of the United States, for the purpose of aiding and assisting such subjects in their attempts to avoid criminal liability;

8. making or causing to be made false or misleading public statements for the purpose of deceiving the people of the United States into believing that a thorough and complete investigation had been conducted with respect to allegations of misconduct on the part of personnel of the executive branch of the United States and personnel of the Committee for the Re-election of the President, and that there was no involvement of such personnel in such misconduct: or

9. endeavoring to cause prospective defendants, and individuals duly tried and convicted, to expect favored treatment and consideration in return for their silence or false testimony, or rewarding individuals for their silence or false testimony.

In all of this, Richard M. Nixon has acted in a manner contrary to his trust as President and subversive of constitutional government, to the great prejudice of the cause of law and justice and to the manifest injury of the people of the United States.

Wherefore Richard M. Nixon, by such conduct, warrants impeachment and trial, and removal from office.

Adopted 27-11.

Article 2

Using the powers of the office of President of the United States, Richard M. Nixon, in violation of his constitutional oath faithfully to execute the office of President of the United States and, to the best of his ability, preserve, protect, and defend the Constitution of the United States, and in disregard of his constitutional duty to take care that the laws be faithfully executed, has repeatedly engaged in conduct violating the constitutional rights of citizens, impairing the due and proper administration of justice and the conduct of lawful inquiries, or contravening the laws governing agencies of the executive branch and the purposes of these agencies.

This conduct has included one or more of the following:

1. He has, acting personally and through his subordinates and agents, endeavored to obtain from the Internal Revenue Service, in violation of the constitutional rights of citizens, confidential information contained in income tax returns for purposes not authorized by law, and to cause, in violation of the constitutional rights of citizens, income tax audits or other income tax investigations to be initiated or conducted in a discriminatory manner.

2. He misused the Federal Bureau of Investigation, the Secret Service, and other executive personnel, in violation or disregard of the constitutional rights of citizens, by directing or authorizing such agencies or personnel to

conduct or continue electronic surveillance or other investigations for purposes unrelated to national security, the enforcement of laws, or any other lawful function of his office; he did direct, authorize, or permit the use of information obtained thereby for purposes unrelated to national security, the enforcement of laws, or any other lawful function of his office; and he did direct the conceal-ment of certain records made by the Federal Bureau of Investigation of electronic surveillance.

3. He has, acting personally and through his subordinates and agents, in violation or disregard of the constitutional rights of citizens, authorized and permitted to be main-tained a secret investigative unit within the office of the President, financed in part with money derived from cam-paign contributions, which unlawfully utilized the resources of the Central Intelligence Agency, engaged in covert and unlawful activities, and attempted to prejudice the constitutional right of an accused to a fair trial.

4. He has failed to take care that the laws were faithfully exe-cuted by failing to act when he knew or had reason to know that his close subordinates endeavored to impede and frustrate lawful inquiries by duly constituted execu-tive, judicial and legislative entities concerning the unlawful entry into the headquarters of the Democratic National Committee, and the cover-up thereof, and con-cerning other unlawful activities including those relating

to the confirmation of Richard Kleindienst as Attorney General of the United States, the electronic surveillance of private citizens, the break-in into the offices of Dr. Lewis Fielding, and the campaign financing practices of the Committee to Re-elect the President.

5. In disregard of the rule of law, he knowingly misused the executive power by interfering with agencies of the executive branch, including the Federal Bureau of Investigation, the Criminal Division, and the Office of Watergate Special Prosecution Force, of the Department of Justice, and the Central Intelligence Agency, in violation of his duty to take care that the laws be faithfully executed.

In all of this, Richard M. Nixon has acted in a manner contrary to his trust as President and subversive of constitutional government, to the great prejudice of the cause of law and justice and to the manifest injury of the people of the United States.

Wherefore Richard M. Nixon, by such conduct, warrants impeachment and trial, and removal from office.

Adopted 28-10.

Article 3
In his conduct of the office of President of the United States, Richard M. Nixon, contrary to his oath faithfully to execute

the office of President of the United States and, to the best of his ability, preserve, protect, and defend the Constitution of the United States, and in violation of his constitutional duty to take care that the laws be faithfully executed, has failed without lawful cause or excuse to produce papers and things as directed by duly authorized subpoenas issued by the Committee on the Judiciary of the House of Representatives on April 11, 1974, May 15, 1974, May 30, 1974, and June 24, 1974, and willfully disobeyed such subpoenas. The subpoenaed papers and things were deemed necessary by the Committee in order to resolve by direct evidence fundamental, factual questions relating to Presidential direction, knowledge or approval of actions demonstrated by other evidence to be substantial grounds for impeachment of the President. In refusing to produce these papers and things Richard M. Nixon, substituting his judgment as to what materials were necessary for the inquiry, interposed the powers of the Presidency against the lawful subpoenas of the House of Representatives, thereby assuming to himself functions and judgments necessary to the exercise of the sole power of impeachment vested by the Constitution in the House of Representatives.

In all of this, Richard M. Nixon has acted in a manner contrary to his trust as President and subversive of constitutional government, to the great prejudice of the cause of law and justice, and to the manifest injury of the people of the United States.

Wherefore, Richard M. Nixon, by such conduct, warrants impeachment and trial, and removal from office.

Adopted 21-17.

APPENDIX F

Article of Impeachment against Richard M. Nixon on Cambodia, *Not Adopted*

Article Four

In his conduct of the office of President of the United States, Richard M. Nixon, in violation of his constitutional oath faithfully to execute the office of President of the United States and, to the best of his ability, preserve, protect, and defend the Constitution of the United States, and in disregard of his constitutional duty to take care that the laws be faithfully executed, on and subsequent to March 17, 1969, authorized, ordered, and ratified the concealment from the Congress of the facts and the submission to the Congress of false and misleading statements concerning the existence, scope and nature of American bombing operations in Cambodia in derogation of the power of the Congress to declare war, to make appropriations, and to raise and support armies, and by such conduct warrants impeachment and trial and removal from office.

Not adopted, 26–12.

Appendix G
Excerpts from Opinion of Justice Jackson, U.S. Supreme Court, on Presidential Powers, *The Steel Seizure Case*

SUPREME COURT OF THE UNITED STATES
Youngstown Sheet & Tube Co. v. *Sawyer,* 343 U.S. 579 (1952)
(on Presidential Powers and their limitations)

MR. JUSTICE JACKSON, concurring in . . . the opinion of the Court.

Presidential powers are not fixed but fluctuate depending upon their disjunction or conjunction with those of Congress. We may well begin by a somewhat over-simplified grouping of practical situations. . . .

1. When the President acts pursuant to an express or implied authorization of Congress, his authority is at its maximum, for it includes all that he possesses in his own right plus all that Congress can delegate. . . .

2. When the President acts in absence of either a congressional grant or denial of authority, he can only rely upon his own independent powers. . . .

3. When the President takes measures incompatible with the expressed or implied will of Congress, his power is at its lowest ebb, for then he can rely only upon his own

constitutional powers minus any constitutional powers of
Congress over the matter. . . .

Into which of these classifications does this executive seizure
of the steel industry fit? It is eliminated from the first, for it is
conceded that no congressional authorization exists. . . .

It seems clearly eliminated from [the second category]
because Congress has [enacted] . . . three statutory policies
inconsistent with this seizure. . . .

This leaves the current seizure to be justified only by the
severe tests under the third grouping. . . . In short, we can
sustain the President only by holding that seizure of such
strike-bound industries is within his domain and beyond control by Congress. . . .

The example of such unlimited executive power that must
have most impressed the forefathers was the prerogative exer-
cised by George III, and the description of its evils in the
Declaration of Independence leads me to doubt that they
were creating their new Executive in his image. . . . And, if we
seek instruction from our own times, we can match it only
from the executive powers in those governments we disparag-
ingly describe as totalitarian. . . .

The clause on which the Government next relies is that "The
President shall be Commander in Chief of the Army and

Navy of the United States. . . ." These cryptic words have given rise to some of the most persistent controversies in our constitutional history. . . .

Assuming that we are in a war . . . does that empower the Commander in Chief to seize industries he thinks necessary to supply our army? The Constitution expressly places in Congress power "to raise and support Armies." . . . This certainly lays upon Congress primary responsibility for supplying the armed forces. Congress alone controls the raising of revenues and their appropriation, and may determine in what manner . . . they shall be spent for military . . . procurement. . . .

There are indications that the Constitution did not contemplate that the title Commander in Chief of the Army and Navy will constitute him also Commander in Chief of the country, its industries and its inhabitants. He has no monopoly of "war powers," whatever they are. While Congress cannot deprive the President of the command of the army and navy, only Congress can provide him an army or navy to command. It is also empowered to make rules for the "Government and Regulation of land and naval Forces," by which it may, to some unknown extent, impinge upon even command functions.

That military powers of the Commander in Chief were not to supersede representative government of internal affairs seems obvious from the Constitution and from elementary American history. . . .

It also was expressly left to Congress to "provide for calling forth the Militia to execute the Laws of the Union, suppress Insurrections and repel Invasions. . . . Such a limitation on the command power, written at a time when the militia, rather than a standing army, was contemplated as the military weapon of the Republic, underscores the Constitution's policy that Congress, not the Executive, should control utilization of the war power as an instrument of domestic policy. . . .

His command power . . . is subject to limitations consistent with a constitutional Republic whose law and policymaking branch is a representative Congress. The purpose of lodging dual titles in one man was to insure that the civilian would control the military, not to enable the military to subordinate the presidential office. No penance would ever expiate the sin against free government of holding that a President can escape control of executive powers by law through assuming his military role. . . .

The appeal, however, that we declare the existence of inherent powers . . . to meet an emergency asks us to do . . . something the forefathers omitted. They knew what emergencies were, knew the pressures they engender for authoritative action, knew, too, how they afford a ready pretext for usurpation. . . . Aside from suspension of the writ of habeas corpus . . . . , they made no express provision for exercise of extraordinary authority because of a crisis. I do not think we rightfully may so amend their work, and, I am not convinced it would be wise to do so. . . .

Emergency powers are consistent with free government only when their control is lodged elsewhere than in the Executive who exercises them. . . .

I am quite unimpressed with the argument that we should affirm possession of [large presidential emergency powers] without statute. Such power either has no beginning or it has no end. . . . I am not alarmed that it would plunge us straightway into dictatorship, but it is at least a step in that wrong direction. . . .

With all its defects, delays and inconveniences, men have discovered no technique for long preserving free government except that the Executive be under the law, and that the law be made by parliamentary deliberations.

Appendix H
Excerpts from the Geneva Conventions

Convention (III) Relative to the Treatment of Prisoners of War. Geneva, 12 August 1949.

Art 3. In the case of armed conflict not of an international character occurring in the territory of one of the High Contracting Parties, each Party to the conflict shall be bound to apply, as a minimum, the following provisions:

(1) Persons taking no active part in the hostilities, including members of armed forces who have laid down their arms and

those placed hors de combat by sickness, wounds, detention, or any other cause, shall in all circumstances be treated humanely, without any adverse distinction founded on race, colour, religion or faith, sex, birth or wealth, or any other similar criteria. To this end the following acts are and shall remain prohibited at any time and in any place whatsoever with respect to the above-mentioned persons:

(a) violence to life and person, in particular murder of all kinds, mutilation, cruel treatment and torture;
(b) taking of hostages;
(c) outrages upon personal dignity, in particular, humiliating and degrading treatment;
(d) the passing of sentences and the carrying out of executions without previous judgment pronounced by a regularly constituted court affording all the judicial guarantees which are recognized as indispensable by civilized peoples. . . .

Art 4. A. Prisoners of war, in the sense of the present Convention, are persons belonging to one of the following categories, who have fallen into the power of the enemy: (1) Members of the armed forces of a Party to the conflict, as well as members of militias or volunteer corps forming part of such armed forces. . . .

Art 5. The present Convention shall apply to the persons referred to in Article 4 from the time they fall into the power of the enemy and until their final release and repatriation.

Should any doubt arise as to whether persons, having committed a belligerent act and having fallen into the hands of the enemy, belong to any of the categories enumerated in Article 4, such persons shall enjoy the protection of the present Convention until such time as their status has been determined by a competent tribunal.

Art 13. Prisoners of war must at all times be humanely treated. Any unlawful act or omission by the Detaining Power causing death or seriously endangering the health of a prisoner of war in its custody is prohibited, and will be regarded as a serious breach of the present Convention. . . .

Likewise, prisoners of war must at all times be protected, particularly against acts of violence or intimidation and against insults and public curiosity.

Measures of reprisal against prisoners of war are prohibited.

Art 14. Prisoners of war are entitled in all circumstances to respect for their persons and their honour. . . .

Art 130. Grave breaches . . . shall be those involving any of the following acts, if committed against persons . . . protected by the Convention: wilful killing, torture or inhuman treatment, including biological experiments, wilfully causing great suffering or serious injury to body or health . . . , or wilfully depriving a prisoner of war of the rights of a fair and regular trial prescibed in this Convention.

Select Sources

BOOKS

Baker, Peter. *The Breach: Inside the Impeachment and Trial of William Jefferson Clinton*. New York: Berkley Books, 2001.

Beevor, Antony, and Luba Vinogradova eds. *A Writer At War: Vasily Grossman with the Red Army, 1941–1945*. New York: Pantheon Books, 2006.

Berger, Raoul. *Impeachment: The Constitutional Problems*. Cambridge, MA: Harvard University Press, 1973.

Bernstein, Carl and Bob Woodward. *All the President's Men*. New York: Simon & Schuster, 1974.

Black, Charles L. Jr. *Impeachment: A Handbook*. New Haven: Yale University Press, 1974.

Bremer, L. Paul III, Malcolm McConnell. *My Year in Iraq: The Struggle to Build a Future of Hope*. New York: Simon & Schuster, 2006.

Center for Constitutional Rights. *Articles of Impeachment Against George W. Bush*. Hoboken: Melville House Publishing, 2006.

Clarke, Richard A. *Against All Enemies: Inside America's War on Terror.* New York: Free Press, 2004.

Clinton, Bill. *My Life.* New York: Alfred A. Knopf, 2004.

Committee on the Judiciary, House of Representatives, Ninety-third Congress, 2nd Session. *Impeachment of Richard M. Nixon, President of the United States: The Final Report of the Committee on the Judiciary, House of Representatives,Peter W. Rodino, Jr., Chairman.* New York: Viking Press, 1975.

Cooley, Thomas M. *The General Principles of Constitutional Law in the United States of America.* Boston: Little, Brown, and Company 1898 (on the Constitution Society Web site at http://www.constitution.org/cmt/tmc/pcl.htm, accessed May 31, 2006).

Corn, David. *The Lies of George W. Bush: Mastering the Politics of Deception.* New York: Crown Publishers, 2003.

Danner, Mark. *Torture and Truth: America, Abu Ghraib, and the War on Terror.* New York: New York Review Books, 2004.

Dean, John W. *Worse than Watergate: The Secret Presidency of George W. Bush.* New York: Little, Brown and Company, 2004.

Debate on Articles of Impeachment, Hearings of the Committee on the Judiciary, House of Representatives. Washington, D.C.: U.S. Government Printing Office, 1974.

Diamond, Larry. *Squandered Victory: The American Occupation and the Bungled Effort to Bring Democracy to Iraq.* New York: Times Books, 2005.

Ehrlich, Walter. *Presidential Impeachment: An American Dilemma.* Saint Charles, MO: Forum Press, 1974.

Farrand, Max ed. *The Records of the Federal Convention of 1787.* New Haven: Yale University Press 1966 (on the Web at http://lcWeb2.loc.gov/ammem/amlaw/lwfr.html, accessed May 31, 2006).

Gerhardt, Michael J. *The Federal Impeachment Process: A Constitutional and Historical Analysis.* Chicago: The University of Chicago Press, 2000.

Gordon, Michael R. and Bernard E. Trainor. *Cobra II: The Inside Story of the Invasion and Occupation of Iraq.* New York: Pantheon Books, 2006.

Greenberg, Karen J. and Joshua L. Dratel eds. *The Torture Papers: The Road to Abu Ghraib.* Cambridge University Press, 2005.

Greenberg, Karen J., ed. *The Torture Debate in America.* New York: Cambridge University Press, 2006.

Hamilton, Alexander, John Jay, and James Madison. *The Federalist: A Commentary on the Constitution of the United States. New York:* Modern Library.

Hersh, Seymour M. *Chain of Command: The Road from 9/11 to Abu Ghraib.* New York: HarperCollins, 2004.

Holtzman, Elizabeth with Cynthia L. Cooper. *Who Said It Would Be Easy: One Woman's Life in the Political Arena.* New York: Arcade, 1996.

Impeachment of Richard M. Nixon, President of the United States: The Final Report of the Committee on the Judiciary, House of Representatives, Peter W. Rodino, Jr., Chairman; With an introduction by R.W. Apple, Jr., of the New York Times. New York: The Viking Press, 1975.

The Impeachment and Trial of President Clinton: The Official Transcripts, from the House Judiciary Committee Hearings to the Senate Trial; Intro-

duction by Michael R. Beschloss. New York: Times Books, Random House, 1999.

Jefferson, Thomas, with an introduction by Wilbur Samuel Howell. *A Manual of Parliamentary Practice: For the Use of the Senate of the United States,* 1812, on the Web at www.constitution.org/tj/tj-mpp.htm, accessed May 2006.

Karpinski, Janis with Steven Strausser. *One Woman's Army: The Commanding General of Abu Ghraib Tells Her Story.* New York: Miramax Books, 2005.

Lindorff, Dave and Barbara Olshansky. *The Case for Impeachment: The Legal Argument for Removing President George W. Bush from Office.* New York: Thomas Dunne Books, 2006.

Rehnquist, William H. *Grand Inquests: The Historic Impeachments of Justice Samuel Chase and President Andrew Johnson.* New York: Quill, William Morrow, 1999.

Risen, James. *State of War: The Secret History of the CIA and the Bush Administration.* New York: Free Press, 2006.

Sofaer, Abraham D. *War, Foreign Affairs, and Constitutional Power: The Origins.* Cambridge MA: Ballinger Publishing Co., 1976.

Sands, Philippe. *Lawless World.* London: Penguin Books, 2006.

Schlesinger, Arthur M., Jr. *The Imperial Presidency.* New York: Popular Library, 1974.

Suskind, Ron. *The Price of Loyalty: George W. Bush, the White House, and the Education of Paul O'Neill.* New York: Simon & Schuster, 2004.

The Staff of the *New York Times. The End of a Presidency*. New York: Bantam Books, 1974

The 9/11 Commission Report: Final Report of the National Commission on Terrorist Acts Upon the United States. Washington, D.C.: U.S. Government Printing Office [no date].

Woodward, Bob. *Plan of Attack*. New York: Simon & Schuster, 2004.

REPORTS

American Bar Association Accuses President Bush of Violating Both the Constitution and Federal Law, February 13, 2006; on the Web at www.informationclearinghouse.info/article12294.htm, accessed May 2006.

American Bar Association Task Force on Treatment of Enemy Combatants Criminal Justice Section. Section of Individual Rights and Responsibilities. Report to the House of Delegates February 2003; on the Web at http://fl1.findlaw.com/news.findlaw.com/hdocs/docs/aba/abatskforce103rpt.pdf, accessed May 2006.

American Civil Liberties Union, "Enduring Abuse: Torture and Cruel Treatment by the United States at Home and Abroad, Report to UN Committee Against Torture" April 27, 2006; on the Web at www.aclu.org/safefree/torture/25354pub20060427.html, accessed May 2006.

Bazan, Elizabeth and Jennifer K. Elsea. *Presidential Authority to Conduct Warrantless Electronic Surveillance to Gather Foreign Intelligence Information*. Washington, D.C.: Congressional Research Service, 2006.

Belasco, Amy. *The Cost of Iraq, Afghanistan, and Other Global War on Terror Operations Since 9/11.* Congressional Research Service, April 24, 2006; on the Web at http://72.14.209.104/search?q=cache:jntJFM8VIE4J:www.fas.org/sgp/crs/natsec/RL33110.pdf+congressional+research+service+war+iraq+costs&hl=en&gl=us&ct=clnk&cd=1, accessed June 2006.

Carnegie Endowment for International Peace Report "Weapons of Mass Destruction in Iraq: Evidence and Implications." January, 2004; on the Web at www.carnegieendowment.org/files/Iraq3FullText.pdf, accessed May 2006.

Cirincione, Joseph, Jessica T. Mathews, George Perkovich with Alexis Orton. *WMD in Iraq: Evidence and Implications.* New York: Carnegie Endowment for International Peace, January 2004; on the Web at www.carnegieendowment.org/files/Iraq3FullText.pdf, accessed May 2006.

Committee Against Torture, 36th Session. 1-19 May 2006. Advanced Unedited Version of Consideration of Reports Submitted by States Parties Under Article 19 of the Convention; on the Web at: www.ohchr.org/english/bodies/cat/docs/AdvanceVersions/CAT.C.USA.CO.2.pdf accessed May 2006.

"The Conyers Report", House Democratic Committee Staff: *The Constitution in Crisis: the Downing Street Minutes and Deception, Manipulation, Torture, Retribution and Coverups in the Iraq War* Washington, D.C. 2005; on the Web at www.house.gov/judiciary_democrats/iraqrept.html, accessed on May 2006.

Council on Foreign Relations. *"Iraq: The Day After: Report of an Independent Task-Force,"* Eric P. Schwartz, Project Director Council on Foreign Relations Press, March 2003; on the Web at www.cfr.org, accessed May 2006.

"The Fay Report" Fay, George. "Investigation of the Abu Ghraib Detention Facility and 205th Military Intelligence Brigade." On the Web at http://fl1.

findlaw.com/news.findlaw.com/hdocs/docs/dod/fay82504rpt.pdf, accessed May 2006.

The Human Rights Watch World Report 2006; on the Web at http://hrw.org/wr2k6/, accessed May 2006.

Human Rights Watch, "Getting Away With Torture? Command Responsibility for the U.S. Abuses of Detainees," April 2005 Vol 17, No. 1 G; on the Web at http://www.hrw.org/reports/2005/us0405/ accessed May 2006.

Report of the International Committee of the Red Cross ICRC on the Treatment by the Coalition Forces of Prisoners of War and Other Protected Persons by the Geneva Conventions in Iraq During Arrest, Internment and Interrogation, February 2004; on the Web at www.globalsecurity.org, accessed May 2006.

The "Jones Report": Jones, Anthony R. "Investigation of the Abu Ghraib Prison and 205th Military Intelligence Brigade." On the Web at http://fl1. findlaw.com/news.findlaw.com/hdocs/docs/dod/fay82504rpt.pdf, accessed May 2006.

Kosiak, Steven M. "Three Years Later: The Cost of US Military Operations in Iraq," Center for Strategic and Budgetary Assessments, March 20, 2006; on the Web at www.csbaonline.org, accessed June 2006.

National Intelligence Council, *Principal Challenges in Post-Saddam Iraq*, excerpted in "Early Analyses: 'A Long, Difficult and Probably Turbulent Process,' "*New York Times*, October 20, 2004, Section A., p12.

The Project for the New American Century's Report: "Rebuilding America's Defenses." September 2000; on the Web at http://newamericancentury.org/RebuildingAmericasDefenses.pdf, accessed May 2006.

"The Schlesinger Report," *The Final Report of the Independent Panel To Review DOD Detention Operations*, August 2004; on the Web at www.findlaw.com/, accessed May 2006.

The Final Report of the Select Bipartisan Committee to Investigate the Preparation for and Response to Hurricane Katrina: *House Report on Katrina: A Failure of Initiative*, February 15, 2006 Washington, D.C.: U.S. Government Printing Office 2006; on the Web at katrina.house.gov/full_katrina_report.htm, accessed May 2006.

Report of the Senate Committee on Homeland Security and Governmental Affairs: *Hurricane Katrina: A Nation Still Unprepared*, May 2006; on the Web at http://hsgac.senate.gov, accessed May 2006.

Shamsi, Hina, Deborah Pearlstein, ed., *Command's Responsibility, Detainee Deaths in U.S Custody in Iraq and Afghanistan*, Human Rights First, February, 2006; on the Web at www.humanrightsfirst.org, accessed May 2006.

The "Taguba Report" on Treatment of Abu Ghraib Prisoners in Iraq: Article 15-6 Investigation of the 800th Military Police Brigade; on the Web at http://news.findlaw.com/cnn/docs/iraq/tagubarpt.html, accessed May 2006.

Total Information Awareness TIA, Introduction, Electronic Privacy Information Network; on the Web at www.epic.org/privacy/profiling/tia/, accessed May 2006.

Report on the U.S. Intelligence Community's Prewar Intelligence Assessments on Iraq, Select Committee on Intelligence, U.S Senate. July 7, 2004; on the Web at http://fl1.findlaw.com/news.findlaw.com/hdocs/docs/iraq/sic70904iraqrpt.pdf, accessed May 2006.

DOCUMENTS

President George W. Bush, Letter to Congress on Military Action in Iraq, March 18, 2003; on the Web at www.whitehouse.gov/news/releases/2003/03/20030319-1.html, accessed May 2006.

Memorandum from President George W. Bush Regarding the "Humane Treatment of al Qaeda and Taliban Detainees," February 7, 2002; on the Web at http://www.gwu.edu/~nsarchiv/NSAEBB/NSAEBB127/02.02.07.pdf, accessed May 2006.

Bush Administration's Legal Debate Over Torture, Interrogation Policies, Treatment of Enemy Combatants and Detainees, and the Applicability of Prisoner of War Status," January 25, 2002; on the Web at news.findlaw.com/hdocs/docs/torture/powtorturememos.html, accessed May 2006.

President Jimmy Carter Statement on Signing S.1566 Into Law, Foreign Intelligence Surveillance Act, October 25, 1978 on the Web at www.cnss.org/Carter.pdf, accessed May 2006.

Statement by President William J. Clinton-Law H.R. 3680, War Crimes Act, August 21, 1996; on the Web at http://clinton6.nara.gov/1996/08/1996-08-21-president-statement-on-signing-war-crimes-act-of.html, accessed May 2006.

Letter to President William J. Clinton, January 26, 1998; on the Web at http://newamericancentury.org/iraqclintonletter.htm, accessed May 2006. Memorandum for James B. Comey Deputy Attorney General. "Legal Standards Applicable Under 18 U.S.C 2340-2340A;" on the Web at www.usdoj.gov/olc/18usc23402340a2.htm, accessed May 2006.

"Conyers Resolution," House Resolution 635 "Creating a Select Committee to Investigate the Administration's intent to go to war before congressional authorization, manipulation of pre-war intelligence, encouraging and countenancing torture, retaliating against critics, and to make recommendations regarding ground for possible impeachment," December 18, 2005; on the Web at http://thomas.loc.gov.

Downing Street and Other Memos; on the Web at www.downingstreet-memo.com, accessed May 2006.

Presidential Papers of Dwight David Eisenhower Document #1536, August 1, 1955; on the Web at www.eisenhowermemorial.org, accessed May 2006.

Foreign Intelligence Surveillance Act Orders 1979-2005, Electronic Privacy Information Center; on the Web at www.epic.org/privacy/wiretap/stats/fisa_stats.html, accessed May 2006.

Fox, Gregory H. "The Occupation of Iraq," *Georgetown Journal of International Law*, January 1, 2005.

Geneva Convention Relative to the Treatment of Prisoners of War. Adopted August 12, 1949; on the Web at www.unhchr.ch/html/menu3/b/91.htm, accessed May 2006.

Memorandum for the President from Alberto R. Gonzales. "Decision Re: Application of the Geneva Convention on Prisoners of War to the Conflict with Al Qaeda and the Taliban," January 25, 2002; on the Web at www.gwu.edu/~nsarchiv/NSAEBB/NSAEBB127/02.01.25.pdf, accessed May 2006.

Letter from Attorney General Alberto Gonzales to the Honorable Arlen Specter in response to the "Wartime Executive Power and the National Security Agency's Surveillance Authority" hearing, February 28, 2006; on the Web at www.fas.org/irp/congress/2006_hr/022806gonzales.pdf, accessed May 2006.

Government Documents on Torture Freedom of Information Act, American Civil Liberties Union, April 29, 2005; on the Web at www.aclu.org/intlhumanrights/gen/13794res20050429.html, accessed May 2006.

Hamdi v. Rumsfeld, 542 U.S. 507 (2004).

Response from Law Professors and Former Government Officials to the Justice Department's December 22 letter on January 9, 2006; on the Web at www.fas.org/irp/agency/doj/fisa/doj-response.pdf, accessed May 2006.

Law Professors and Former Government Officials Response to DOJ Domestic Surveillance Memorandum from their January 9, 2006 letter, February 2, 2006; on the Web at jurist.law.pitt.edu/nsascholarsreply.pdf, accessed May 2006.

National Intelligence Estimate, October 2002, on Iraq, Declassified Excerpts; on the Web at www.fas.org/irp/cia/product/iraq-wmd.html, accessed May 2006.

State Department Memorandum, "Sale of Niger Uranium to Iraq Unlikely," March 4, 2002; on the Web at www.judicialwatch.org/archive/niger-uranium.pdf, accessed May 2006.

State Department Memorandum from Carl W. Ford to Under Secretary Grossman, June 10, 2003; on the Web at www.nysun.com/pics/31062_1.php, accessed May 2006.

Application of Yamashita, 327 U.S. 1 (1946).

Youngstown Co. v. Sawyer. 343 U.S. 579 (1952).

Memorandum to Counsel to the President, Assistant to the President for National Security Affairs from Secretary of State Colin L. Powell. "Draft Decision Memorandum for the President on The Applicability of the Geneva Convention to the Conflict in Afghanistan." January 25, 2002; on the Web at http://msnbc.com/modules/newsweek/pdf/powell_memo.pdf, accessed May 2006.

The secret Downing Street memo, The Sunday Times, May 1, 2005; on the Web at www.timesonline.co.uk/article/0,,2087-1593607,00.html, accessed May 2006.

Special Counsel Investigation, Indictment of I. Lewis Libby; on the Web at www.usdoj.gov/usao/iln/osc/documents/libby_indictment_28102005.pdf, accessed May 2006.

Special Counsel Investigation of Patrick Fitzgerald, Legal Documents; on the Web at www.usdoj.gov/usao/iln/osc/legal_proceedings.html, accessed May 2006.

Summary of International and U.S Law Prohibiting Torture and Other Ill-Treatment of Persons in Custody. Human Rights Watch. May 24, 2004; on the Web at http://hrw.org/english/docs/2004/05/24/sint8614_txt.htm, accessed May 2006.

HEARINGS

Testimony of U.S. Secretary of Defense Donald H. Rumsfeld before the Senate Armed Services Committee regarding Iraq Transcript, September 19, 2002; on the Web at www.defenselink.mil/speeches/2002/s20020919-secdef2.html, accessed May 2006.

U.S Senate Armed Services Committee Hearing on FY 2004 Defense Authorization, transcript, February 25, 2003.

Hearing of the Senate Committee on Appropriations, President's Fiscal 2004 Supplemental Request for Iraq and Afghanistan, September 24, 2003; on the Web at. www.iraqwatch.org/government/US/HearingsPreparedstatements/us-senapprop-transcript-092403.htm, accessed May 2006.

Testimony of Secretary of Defense Donald H. Rumsfeld Before the Senate and House Armed Services Committees, May 7, 2004; on the Web at http://armedservices.senate.gov/statemnt/2004/May/Rumsfeld.pdf, accessed May 2006.

Hearing Before the Senate Judiciary Committee on "Wartime Executive Power and the National Security Agency's Surveillance Authority" February 6, 2006; on the Web at www.washingtonpost.com/wpdyn/content/article/2006/02/06/AR2006020600931.html, accessed May 2006.

SPEECHES, BRIEFINGS

President George W. Bush Speech to the UN, September 12, 2002; on Web at www.whitehouse.gov/news/releases/2002/09/200209121.html, accessed May 2006.

President George W. Bush, Speech on Iraq in Cincinnati, October 7, 2002; on Web at www.whitehouse.gov/news/releases/2002/10/200210078.html, accessed May 2006.

President George W. Bush State of Union Address January 28, 2003; on the Web at www.whitehouse.gov/news/releases/2003/01/20030128-19.html, accessed May 2006.

President Says Saddam Hussein Must Leave in 24 Hours, March 17, 2003; on the Web at www.whitehouse.gov/news/releases/2003/03/20030317-7.html, accessed May 2006.

President Bush Announces Major Combat Operations in Iraq Ended, Remarks by the President from the USS *Abraham Lincoln* at Sea Off the Coast of San Diego, May 1, 2003; on the Web at www.whitehouse.gov/news/releases/2003/05/20030501-15.html, accessed May 2006.

President Outlines Six Point Plan for the Economy, Kansas Convention Center, Kansas City, Missouri, September 4, 2003; on the Web at www.whitehouse.gov/news/releases/2003/09/20030904-5.html, accessed May 2006.

President Bush: Information Sharing, Patriot Act Vital to Homeland Security, Remarks by the President in a Conversation on the USA Patriot Act, Buffalo, NY, April 20, 2004; on the Web at www.whitehouse.gov/news/releases/2004/04/20040420-2.html, accessed May 2006.

President's Remarks at Ask President Bush Event, Fond Du Lac, WI, July 14, 2004; on the Web at http://www.whitehouse.gov/news/releases/2004/07/20040714-11.html, accessed May 2006.

President Discusses Patriot Act, Columbus, OH, June 9, 2005; on the Web at www.whitehouse.gov/news/releases/2005/06/20050609-2.html, accessed May 2006.

President George W. Bush State of Union Address, January 31 2006; on the Web at www.whitehouse.gov/stateoftheunion/2006/index.html, accessed May 2006.

President Discusses War on Terror and Operation Iraqi Freedom, Cleveland, Ohio, March 20, 2006; on the Web at www.whitehouse.gov/news/releases/2006/03/20060320-7.html, accessed May 2006.

President George W. Bush, White House Press Conference of the President, March 21, 2006; on the Web at www.whitehouse.gov/news/releases/2006/03/print/20060321-4.html, accessed May 2006.

President Bush Discusses Global War on Terror at The John Hopkins University, Washington, D.C., April 10, 2006; on the Web at www.whitehouse.gov/news/releases/2006/04/20060410-1.html, accessed May 2006.

Briefing of President Bush about Hurricane Katrina on August 28, 2005, transcript on the Web at www.usatoday.com/news/katrinatranscript-0828.pdf, accessed May 2006.

Carnegie Endowment for International Peace Discussion Topic: The Report "Weapons of Mass Destruction in Iraq: Evidence and Implications," January 8, 2004; on the Web at www.carnegieendowment.org/files/wmdtranscript.pdf, accessed May 2006.

Vice President Speaks at VFW 103rd National Convention, August 26, 2002; on the Web at http://www.whitehouse.gov/news/releases/2002/08/20020826.html

Remarks of Senator Russ Feingold Introducing a Resolution to Censure President George W. Bush. March 13, 2006; on the Web at www.feingold.senate.gov/statements/06/03/2006313.html, accessed May 2006.

Press Conference of Special Prosecutor Patrick Fitzgerald, October 28, 2005; on the Web at www.usdoj.gov/usao/iln/osc/documents/2005_10_28_fitzgerald_press_conference.pdf, accessed May 2006.

Press Briefing by Attorney General Alberto Gonzales and General Michael Hayden; on the Web at www.whitehouse.gov/news/releases/2005/12/20051219-1.html, accessed May 2006.

Remarks by General Michael V. Hayden. Address to the National Press Club: "What American Intelligence and Especially the NSA Have been Doing to Defend the Nation" January 23, 2006; on the Web at www.fas.org/irp/news/2006/01/hayden012306.html, accessed May 2006.

Statement of Kate Martin, Director, Center for National Security Studies Before the Members of the Committees of the Judiciary and the Select Committee on Intelligence House of Representatives on the Scope of Executive Power Since 9/11, January 20, 2006; on the Web at http://cnss.org/MartinNSAstatement%20.doc, accessed May 2006.

Secretary of State Colin Powell, Speech to UN February 5, 2003; on the Web at www.whitehouse.gov/news/releases/2003/02/20030205-1.html, accessed May 2006.

Speech of Donald Rumsfeld, "Beyond Nation Building," February 14, 2003; on the Web at www.defenselink.mil/speeches/2003/sp20030214-secdef0023.html, accessed May 2006.

Senior Administration Official Holds Background Briefing on Weapons of Mass Destruction in Iraq, as Released by The White House, July 18. 2003; on the Web at http://fas.org, accessed May 2006.

ARTICLES, STORIES, NEWS REPORTS, INTERVIEWS

ACLU Press Release, "New Documents Provide Further Evidence That Senior Officials Approved Abuse of Prisoners at Guantánamo," February 23, 2006; on the Web at www.aclu.org/intlhumanrights/gen/24249prs 20060223.html, accessed May 2006.

Terry J. Allen, Interview with Central Intelligence Agency spokesperson, Re: Investigations or discipline actions against CIA employees for detainee abuse, June 24th 2006.

Charles Babington and Dan Eggen,"Gonzales Seeks to Clarify Testimony on Spying," Washington Post, March 1, 2006, A08.

Lolita C. Baldor, "Rumsfeld Reveals Split Over Interrogations," *Associated Press*, May 17, 2006; on the Web www.washingtonpost.com/wp-dyn/content/article/2006/05/17/AR2006051701240_pf.html, accessed May 2006.

Neela Banerjee and Ariel Hart, "Soldiers Saw Refusing Order as Their Last Stand," *The New York Times*, October 18, 2004, A1.

Emily Bazelon, "From Bagram to Abu Ghraib," *Mother Jones*, March/April 2005 issue. http://www.motherjones.com accessed May 2006.

Drake Bennett, "The other insurgency," *Boston Globe*, April 16, 2006; on the Web at www.boston.com/news/globe/ideas/articles/2006/04/16/the_other_insurgency/, accessed May 2006.

Lowell Bergman, Eric Lichtblau, Scott Shane, and Don Van Natta Jr., "Spy Agency Data After Sept. 11 Led F.B.I. to Dead Ends," *The New York Times*, January 17, 2006, A1.

David Brooks, "Rumsfeld's Blinkers," *The New York Times*, March 16, 2006, A27.

Elisabeth Bumiller, "Bush Sees No Need for Law To Approve Eavesdropping," *The New York Times*, January 27, 2006.

"Bush: 'I'm the decider on Rumsfeld," CNN.com, April 18, 2006; on the Web at www.cnn.com/2006/POLITICS/04/18/rumsfeld, accessed May 2006.

Former President George H.W Bush and Brent Scowcroft, "Why We Didn't Remove Saddam," *Time*, March 2, 1998, p. .31.

Leslie Cauley, "NSA has Massive Database of Americans' Phone Calls," *USA Today*. May 11, 2006.

Rob Christensen, David Menconi and J. Andrew Curliss, "Novak Inspires Senator's Letter to Bush," *The News and Observer*, December 15, 2005; on the Web at www.newsobserver.com/114/story/378052.html, accessed May 2006.

David Corn, "Now They Tell Us: Postwar Truth and Consequences," *The Nation*, May 19, 2003.

Karen DeYoung, "Bush, Blair Decry Hussein; Iraqi Threat is Real, They Say," *Washington Post*, September 8, 2002, A1.

Karen DeYoung, "Terrorist Attacks Rose Sharply in 2005, State Dept. Says," *Washington Post*, April 29, 2006, A1.

John Diamond and David Jackson, "Bush says Privacy Protected; Sources tell of 'Spider Web' Use," *USA Today*, May 12, 2006.

Jackson Diehl, "How Torture Came Down From the Top," *Washington Post*, August 27, 2004, A21.

Guy Dinmore, "Bush's Pipe Dreams for Reconstructing Iraq," *Financial Times/UK*, January 16, 2004.

Thomas R. Eddlem, "Deceiving Us into War," *The New American*, November 17, 2003; on the Web at www.thenewamerican.com/tna/2003/11-17-2003/war.htm, accessed May 2006.

Michael A. Fletcher, "Bush Defends CIA's Clandestine Prisons," *Washington Post*, November 8, 2005, A15.

Dan Froomkin, "A Dearth of Answers" washingtonpost.com, September 1, 2005; on the Web at www.washingtonpost.com/wpdyn/content/blog/2005/09/01/BL2005090100915.html, accessed May 2006.

Joseph L. Galloway, Jonathan S. Landay, Warren P. Strobel and John Walcott, with research by Tish Wells, "No plan for peace, U.S. invaded Iraq with little concern about aftermath," Knight Ridder Newspapers, October 16, 2004.

Barton Gellman and Dafna Linzer, "A 'Concerted Effort' to Discredit Bush Critic," *Washington Post*, April 9, 2006, A1.

Barton Gellman and Walter Pincus, "Depiction of Threat Outgrew Supporting Evidence." *Washington Post*, August 10, 2003, A1

Josh Gerstein, "Bush Authorized Leak to Times, Libby told Grand Jury," *New York Sun*, April 6, 2006; on the Web at www.nysun.com/timesleak.php, accessed May 2006.

Michael R. Gordon, "Criticizing an Agent of Change as Failing to Adapt," *The New York Times*, April 21, 2006.

"A Guide to the Memos on Torture, *The New York Times* on the Web at www.nytimes.com/ref/international/24MEMO-GUIDE.html, accessed May 2006.

Kathleen Hennessey, "Ex-President Carter: Eavesdropping Illegal," Associated Press, February 7, 2006.

Elizabeth Holtzman, "The Impeachment of George W. Bush," *The Nation*, January 30, 2006.

Elizabeth Holtzman, "Torture and Accountability," *The Nation*, July 18, 2005.

Human Rights Watch Press Release, "World Report 2006: U.S. Policy of Abuse Undermines Rights Worldwide," January 18, 2006; on the Web at http://hrw.org/english/docs/2006/01/13/global12428.htm, accessed May 2006.

Bill Hutchinson, "Ex-Navy Legal Chief Blasts W on Gitmo," *Daily News*, February 20, 2006.

Rear Adm. John D. Hutson (Ret), "Accountability Absent in Prisoner Torture," *St. Paul Pioneer Press*, February 28, 2006; on the Web at http://www.commondreams.org/views06/0228-31.htm, accessed May 2006.

Rear Adm. John D Hutson (Ret), and Brig. Gen. James Cullen (Ret), "From the Top on Down," *Legal Times*, April 18, 2005.

Michael Isikoff, "Memos Reveal War Crimes Warnings," *Newsweek*, May 19, 2004 on the Web at http://msnbc.msn.com/id/4999734/site/newsweek, accessed May 2006.

Derrick Z. Jackson, "The President's War Madness," *Washington Post*, April 3, 2006.
David Johnston and David E. Sanger, "Cheney's Aide Says President Approved Leak," *The New York Times*, April 7, 2006, A1.

Rep. Walter B. Jones Jr. "The United States, A Safe Haven for War Criminals?" *The Hill*, June 19, 1996.

Paul Krugman, "The Crony Fairy," *The New York Times*, April 28, 2006.

Lewis H. Lapham, "The Case for Impeachment" *Harper's Magazine*, March 2006.

Eric Lichtblau, "2002 Memo Doubted Uranium Sale Claim," *The New York Times*, January 18, 2006.

Vernon Loeb and Theola Labbé, "Body Armor Saves U.S Lives in Iraq," *Washington Post*, December 3, 2003.

Tamara Lush, "For forecasting chief, no joy in being right," *St. Petersburg Times*, August 30, 2005.

Jane Mayer, "How an internal effort to ban the abuse and torture of detainees was thwarted," *New Yorker*, February 27, 2006.

Mark Mazzetti, "Prewar Intelligence Ignored, Former C.I.A Official Says," *The New York Times*, April 22, 2006.

Ewen MacAskill, "US postwar Iraq strategy a mess, Blair was told," *The Guardian*, March 14, 2006; on the Web at www.guardian.co.uk/Iraq/Story/0,,1730427,00.html?gusrc=rss, accessed March 2006.

Dana Milbank, "For Bush, Facts Are Malleable; Presidential Tradition of Embroidering Key Assertions Continues," *Washington Post*, October 22, 2002, A1.

Dana Milbank and Walter Pincus, "Bush Aides Disclose Warnings From CIA," *Washington Post*, July 23, 2003, A1.

Judith Miller and Michael R. Gordon, "U.S. Says Hussein Intensifies Quest for A-Bomb Parts," *The New York Times*, September 8, 2002.

David Moniz, "Ex-Army boss: Pentagon won't admit reality in Iraq," *USA Today*, June 3, 2003, A1.

Michael Moss, "Extra Armor Could Have Saved Many Lives, Study Shows," *The New York Times*, January 6, 2006.

Richard Norton-Taylor, "Blair-Bush Deal Before Iraq War Revealed in Secret Memo," The Guardian, February 3, 2006; on the Web at http://politics. guardian.co.uk/iraq/story/0,,1700881,00.html, accessed May 2006.

Robert Novak, "Mission to Niger," Townhall.com, July 14, 2003; on the Web at www.townhall.com/opinion/columns/robertnovak/2003/07/14/ 160881.html, accesssed May 2006.

Brendan Nyhan, "Making Bush Tell the Truth About Iraq," Salon.com, November 8, 2002; on the Web at http://dir.salon.com/story/poli- tics/col/spinsanity/2002/11/08/iraq_truth/index.html, accessed May 2006.

Susan Page, "Furor Erupts Over NSA's Secret Phone Call Database," USA Today, May12-14, 2006, A1.

Paul Pillar, "Intelligence, Policy and the War in Iraq," Foreign Affairs, March/April 2006.

Walter Pincus, "No Link Between Hijackers, Iraq Found, U.S. Says," Washington Post, May 1, 2002, A9.

Walter Pincus, "Spy Agencies Warned of Iraq Resistance," Washington Post, September 9, 2003, A1.

Walter Pincus and Dana Priest, "Bush, Aides Ignored CIA Caveats on Iraq," Washington Post, February 7, 2004, A17.

"Powell Aide: Torture 'guidance' from VP," CNN.com, November 20, 2005; on the Web at www.cnn.com/2005/US/11/20/torture, accessed May 2006.

Dana Priest, "CIA Holds Terror Suspects in Secret Prisons," Washington Post, November 2, 2005, A1.

Dana Priest, "U.S. Not Claiming Iraqi Link to Terror," *Washington Post*, September 10, 2002, A1.

"Prison Interrogators Got F.B.I Warnings," Associated Press, February 24, 2006.

"Red Cross: Guantanamo Tactics 'Tantamount to Torture," Reuters, November 30, 2004.

Tom Regan, "Report: Bush, Blair decided to go to war months before UN Meetings," *Christian Science Monitor*, February 3, 2006; on the Web at www.csmonitor.com/2006/0203/dailyUpdate.html, accessed May 2006.

James Risen and Eric Lichtblau, "Bush Lets U.S. Spy on Callers Without Courts," *The New York Times*, December 16, 2005, A1.

Brian Ross and Richard Esposito, "CIA's Harsh Interrogation Techniques Described," ABC News, November 18, 2005; on the Web at http://abcnews.go.com/WNT/Investigation/story?id=1322866, accessed May 2006.

"Rumsfeld: It Would Be A Short War" CBS, November 15, 2002; on the Web at www.cbsnews.com/stories/2002/11/15/world/main529569.shtml, accessed May 2006.

David E. Sanger and David Barstow, "Iraq Findings Leaked by Cheney's Aide were Disputed," *The New York Times*, April 9, 2006.

David E. Sanger, "Bush Says He Ordered Domestic Spying," *New York Times*, December 18, 2005, A1.

Charlie Savage, "Bush Challenges Hundreds of Laws," *Boston Globe*, April 30, 2006.

Eric Schmitt, "Iraq Abuse Trial Is Again Limited to Lower Ranks," *The New York Times*, March 23, 2006, A1, A22.

Noah Shachtman, "Ex-NSA Chief Assails Bush Taps," Wired.com, May 9, 2006; on the Web at www.wired.com/news/technology/0,70855-0.html, accessed May 2006.

Scott Shane and Eric Lichtblau, "Vice president argued for domestic wiretapping without warrants," *The New York Times*, May 14, 2006.

John Shattuck, "On Abu Ghraib: One Sergeant's Courage a Model for US Leaders," *Christian Science Monitor*, May 16, 2005; on the Web at www.csmonitor.com/2005/0516/p09s02-coop.html, accessed May 2006.

Richard Sisk, "G.I.S Short on Protection, Lack new body armor to stop Iraq sniper attacks," *Daily News*, September 28, 2003.

R. Jeffrey Smith, "Memo Gave Intelligence Bigger Role; Increased Pressure Sought on Prisoners," *Washington Post*, May 21, 2004, A17.

"Soldiers in Iraq Still Buying Their Own Body Armor," Associated Press, March 26, 2004.

Paul South, "A Step Toward Avenging War-Crime Victims; Jones Fought, at an Ex-Pilot's Behest, For a Law to Prosecute War Criminals." *The Virginian-Pilot*, August 29, 1996, B1.

Andrew Sullivan, "We Don't Need a New King George," *Time*, January 23, 2006, 74.

Evan Thomas and John Barry, "Anatomy of a Revolt," *Newsweek*, April 24, 2006.

"The Times and Iraq," *The New York Times*, May 26, 2004.

Jonathan Turley, "The Best possible equipment should include Kevlar and boots," *The Hill*, October 7, 2003.

"US Gives New Details on Iraq, Afghan Abuse Probes." Reuters, May 8, 2006; on the Web at www.afterdowningstreet.org/node/10118, accessed May 2006.

"Video shows Bush, Chertoff warned before Katrina," *USA Today*, March 1, 2006; on the Web at www.usatoday.com/news/nation/2006-03-01-video-katrina-warning_x.htm, accessed May 2006.

Don Van Atta Jr., "Bush Was Set on Path to War, British Memo Says," *The New York Times*, March 27, 2006.

Murray Waas, "What Bush Was Told About Iraq," *The National Journal*, March 2, 2006.

Murray Waas, "Prewar Intelligence: Insulating Bush," *National Journal*, March 30, 2006.

Jonathan Weisman, "Iraq Chaos No Surprise, but Too Few Troops to Quell It," *Washington Post*, April 14, 2003.

Jonathan Weisman, "War Costs Approach $10 Billion a Month," *The San Francisco Chronicle*, April 20, 2006; on the Web at www.sfgate.com, accessed April 2006.

Josh White, "Government Authenticates Photos From Abu Ghraib," *Washington Post*, April 11, 2006; on the Web at www.washingtonpost.com/wpdyn/content/article/2006/04/10/AR2006041001392.html, accessed May 2006.

Josh White, "Army, CIA Agreed on 'Ghost' Prisoners," *Washington Post*, March 11, 2005, A16.

Josh White, "Documents Tell of Brutal Improvisation by GIs," *Washington Post*, August 3, 2005, A1.

Joseph C. Wilson IV, "What I Didn't Find in Africa," *The New York Times*, July 6, 2003.

Pete Yost, "White House Sidesteps Questions on Leak," Associated Press, April 7, 2006; on the Web at http://abcnews.go.com/Politics/wireStory ?id=1818587, accessed May 2006.

BROADCASTS

"Exclusive: Bush Says Focus Must be On People," *Good Morning America*, September 1, 2005; on the Web at http://abcnews.go.com/GMA/Hur-ricaneKatrina/story?id=1086311&page=1, accessed May 2006.

"President Bush Not Worried About Low Approval Ratings," February 28, 2006 ABC News; on the Web at http://abcnews.go.com/WNT/story?id= 1671087&page=1, accessed May 2006.

Vice President Dick Cheney appears on *Meet the Press* with Tim Russert, September 16, 2001; on the Web at www.whitehouse.gov/vicepresident/ news-speeches/speeches/vp20010916.html, accessed May 2006.

Transcript from NBC's *Meet the Press* with Vice President Dick Cheney. December 9, 2001; on the Web at http://www.whitehouse.gov/vicepres-ident/news-speeches/speeches/vp20011209.html

Transcript from NBC's *Meet the Press* with Vice President Dick Cheney and Tim Russert. September 8, 2002; on the Web at http://www.mtholyoke. edu/acad/intrel/bush/meet.htm

Transcript from NBC's "Meet the Press" with Vice President Dick Cheney on War with Iraq, March 16, 2003; on the Web at www.mtholyoke.edu/ acad/intrel/bush/cheneymeetthepress.htm, accessed May 2006.

"Interview with Richard Clarke: What Bush's Ex-Advisor Says about Efforts to Stop War on Terror" *60 Minutes,* March 21, 2004; on the Web at http://www.cbsnews.com/stories/2004/03/19/60minutes/main 607356.shtml

Transcript from interview with United Nations weapons inspector Scott Ritter on CNN's *American Morning,* September 9, 2002; on the Web at http://transcripts.cnn.com/TRANSCRIPTS/0209/09/ltm.14.html

Donald Rumsfeld Participates in Town Meeting with Infinity Radio Stations from the Pentagon with Steve Croft, CBS News. November 14, 2002; on the Web at www.defense.gov/transcripts/2002/t11152002_t1114 rum.html, accessed May 2006.

Transcript from The News Hour with Condoleezza Rice and Jim Lehrer. September 25, 2002; on the Web at http://www.pbs.org/newshour/bb/ international/july-dec02/rice_9-25.html.

"A Spy Speaks Out" *60 Minutes*, April 23, 2006; on the Web at http://www.cbsnews.com/stories/2006/04/21/60minutes/main152774 9.shtml, accessed May 31, 2006.

WEB SITES

American Civil Liberties Union
http://www.aclu.org

Downing Street Memos
http://www.downingstreetmemo.com

Federation of American Scientists
http://www.fas.org

Human Rights First
http://www.humanrightsfirst.org
Human Rights Watch
http://www.hrw.org

Library of Congress, American Memory, Constitutional Debates and Documents http://lcWeb2.loc.gov/ammem/amlaw/lawhome.html
National Security Archives
http://www.gwu.edu/~nsarchiv/

Project to Enforce the Geneva Conventions
http://www.justicescholars.org/pegc/

Watergate Files
http://watergate/info

ACKNOWLEDGMENTS

The authors wish to extend special thanks to Ruth Baldwin, our editor; Katrina vanden Heuvel, editor and publisher of *The Nation*; John Oakes, vice president of Avalon Publishing Group; Hamilton Fish, president of The Nation Institute; Terry J. Allen, senior researcher; and Jennifer Lyons of Lyons & Pande International, LLC, our agent. For their invaluable assistance and support, we also wish to thank Jennifer Clarke, Gen. James Cullen, Michele Martin, Betsy Reed, Perry Applebaum, Robert Sheehan, Minna Schrag, Jim Schweitzer, Judith Ames, Robert Holtzman, Angela Bonavoglia, Francesca Mantani Arkus, Eileen Clancy, Lory Frankel, Bergin O'Malley, Joe Duax, and Sophie Ragsdale. Elizabeth Holtzman also wishes to pay special tribute to her mother, Filia Holtzman (1907–2006), whose inspiration, encouragement, and love made this book possible.